Pierce
1/98

D1607387

Franchise Law Firms
and the Transformation of
Personal Legal Services

Franchise Law Firms and the Transformation of Personal Legal Services

JERRY VAN HOY

QUORUM BOOKS
Westport, Connecticut • London

Library of Congress Cataloging-in-Publication Data

Van Hoy, Jerry.
    Franchise law firms and the transformation of personal legal
services / Jerry Van Hoy.
        p. cm.
    Includes bibliographical references and index.
    ISBN 1-56720-135-0 (alk. paper)
        1. Practice of law—United States.   2. Law firms—United States.
    3. Franchises (Retail trade)—United States.   I. Title.
    KF300.V36   1997
    340'.023—DC21   97-1696

British Library Cataloguing in Publication Data is available.

Library of Congress Catalog Card Number: 97-1696
ISBN: 1-56720-135-0

First published in 1997

Quorum Books, 88 Post Road West, Westport, CT 06881
An imprint of Greenwood Publishing Group, Inc.

Printed in the United States of America

The paper used in this book complies with the
Permanent Paper Standard issued by the National
Information Standards Organization (Z39.48-1984).

10   9   8   7   6   5   4   3   2   1

Contents

Preface

Franchise law firms are different from our common view of what professional organizations are and what professional work is. Rather than providing a kind of collegial "safe haven" for educated workers, franchise law firms adopt technology and organizational styles from mass production industries. Franchise law firms suggest that what is possible in other occupations is also possible in the professions, when the proper conditions arise. This book is about the dynamic between professional markets, innovations in professional organizations and the experiences of professional workers and their clients.

In the professions, franchise law firms are joined by for-profit emergency medical clinics, franchise-style income tax preparation services and a growing number of chains that offer other limited professional services. Although these franchise-style firms do not dominate the professions, they reach large segments of the lay public through television advertising and convenient store-front access. Much of what the public "knows" about the professions is influenced by these firms.

A generation ago, Jerome Carlin presented his classic work *Law-*

yers on Their Own (1994) as a report to the public and the legal profession on the conditions affecting solo practitioners in urban settings. In many ways my work follows in Carlin's footsteps. Not only have I studied lawyers in a similar market setting, but I have focused on the qualitative issues of professional work experiences. Indeed, the research I present on solo and small-firm practitioners is based directly on Carlin's model. His open-ended interview questions remain as insightful and useful as they were over 30 years ago. Carlin's basic approach to studying lawyers also informs my research design for the franchise law firms. Continuing in Carlin's footsteps, I have tried to write this book so that it will be accessible to the public and to lawyers.

I believe this book also contributes to the sociology of the professions by offering a perspective that is different from our common understanding of professional work. Professional work is often viewed as protected from the market forces of capitalism that may lead to experiences of degradation. That perspective is difficult to maintain when we look at personal legal services work in the United States; it is impossible to maintain if we are to understand franchise law firms. The level of control a profession exerts over its market is not determined completely by the exclusion of nonprofessional competitors. Professional practitioners and firms continue to compete among themselves for clients (or employment) and profits. To a great extent it is this intraprofessional competition that defines the markets of existing professions and drives innovations in the delivery of services to clients.

The overall argument of the book, my approach to the legal profession as divided into two major service markets, the theoretical literature I address and the place of franchise law firms in the personal services sector of the legal profession are addressed in Chapter 1. The remainder of the book provides a detailed account of the experiences of attorneys, secretaries and clients at franchise law firms. Chapter 2 describes the basic organization of work at franchise law firms and how that organization is changing in response to changing markets. In many ways secretaries appear to be more important to the operation of branch offices than are lawyers. Chapter 3 analyzes how the lawyers and secretaries who operate local offices serve clients while remaining in roles prescribed by the franchise production systems. This chapter presents a detailed account of how attorneys (and secretaries) sell services to clients that are based on documents and letters easily produced from boilerplate by secretaries. Chapter 4 compares the work practices of sole and small-firm practitioners with those of attorneys employed by franchise law firms. Chapters 5 and 6 address the issues of attorney alienation at franchise law firms. Chapter 5 focuses on how market, organizational and career factors influence attorney interpretations of their experiences in the franchise setting. Chapter 6 extends this analysis by showing how firm organization mediates attitudes toward unions and collective bargaining. Clearly, not everyone associated with franchise law firms is alienated, even if most attorneys are bored with the work. Chapter 7 places the experiences of attorneys and secretaries into an analytic framework that emphasizes the connections between the history of personal legal services work and current market conditions.

Acknowledgments

The study presented in this book began as dissertation research. Over the years many friends and colleagues have helped and encouraged me in a variety of ways. I am indebted to my dissertation committee at Northwestern University, who guided me through the research process as carefully and painlessly as any student might hope. Robert Nelson, my committee chair and graduate studies advisor, managed to find an almost impossible balance between helping to open my eyes as a sociologist and allowing my eyes to wander to new and interesting phenomena to examine. Few graduate advisors are as willing to let students define their own research topics and goals as Bob is. It is hoped that Bob's positive influence upon me is apparent throughout this book.

Arthur Stinchcomb and Bernard Beck, the other members of my dissertation committee, also contributed to this work in distinct ways. Art provided a constant stream of critical comments that forced me to consider new issues and improve my work at all stages of the research and writing process. Bernie diligently listened to numerous stories and potential interpretations of data on a regular basis. The long hours I spent with Bernie were immensely helpful as I sorted through the large amount of data I was collect-ing. I also owe a debt of gratitude to Howard Becker. Howie en-couraged me to follow my instincts as a field researcher even when knowledgeable "insiders" advised me that no one at a franchise firm would talk to me. At a time when I might have abandoned my topic of choice, Howie kept me on track.

I offer special thanks to the many men and women, lawyers, secretaries and managers who spoke with me about their work experiences. Those who allowed me to observe in their offices not only told me about their work but showed me the work process. I could not have completed this study without their help.

A dissertation fellowship from the American Bar Foundation's Project on Professionalism funded my research. During my year in residence I benefited from the wisdom of many colleagues. Bryant Garth, Director of the American Bar Foundation, and Stephen Daniels, Research Fellow, deserve special thanks for offering their many insights into my project. Bryant and Steve read and com-mented on every dissertation chapter I wrote.

Many others also contributed by commenting on chapter drafts. I am indebted to Pam Brandwein, Jerome Carlin, Kelly Devers, Marc Galanter, Terence Halliday, Joanne Martin, Robert Perrucci, Deborah Schleef and Marc Swatez. Diane Clay, Deborah Schleef and Lorrie Wessel accurately and efficiently transcribed many hours of interview tapes. Sarah Elko helped type revisions to chap-ter drafts and the references section of the manuscript.

My parents, Loren and Liesel, deserve much more than the sim-ple thanks I can offer for their years of love, support and enthu-siasm. Even when I chose graduate school over law school their support did not waiver.

Finally, I am most indebted to Ginny and Isaac. Academicians, like many professionals, often spend far too little time at home. They have been more understanding, supportive and loving than I could have hoped for.

1

The Rise of
Franchise Law Firms

The history of the professions traditionally has been a history of economic, intellectual and status monopoly. This book, however, is about a countertrend that is gaining in importance. The legal profession has become an unwitting leader in a movement away from the all-inclusive monopoly back to market competition. The reasons for this movement have to do with the structure of the legal profession and the lifting of restrictions on advertising and other anti-competitive practices. The ramifications are far-reaching and contradictory. Legal services are becoming available to a wider variety of individuals through law firms which organize similar to franchises, target middle-income clients and advertise on television. Yet at the same time, these firms limit the attorney's ability to treat each client individually and craft solutions tailored for the client's particular problems. The franchise style of production adopted by these law firms moves clients through a predetermined sales process that is more focused on selling services than solving client problems.

For lawyers these firms also present a number of dilemmas. Adapting legal practices to the franchise style of organization means that lawyers have to accept the limitations inherent in adding "Mc" (as in McDonald's) to the firm name. The work of lawyers becomes more clerical and sales-oriented at franchise law firms and much less about researching and solving legal problems. Consultations with clients last only about fifteen minutes, as clients are herded through a production system that maximizes productivity and efficiency. Secretaries become almost as important as lawyers, making legal decisions and creating legal documents from computer boilerplate. The pay is low, the hours are long and the work is repetitious and often boring. The franchise law firm asks lawyers to become almost wholly motivated by profit rather than service, often resulting in severe alienation from, and frustration with, franchise law firm work.

Then there is the issue of status and prestige. Attorneys who work for franchise law firms are ridiculed by other members of the profession and even the courts. The franchise-style production system often requires attorneys to set up case files in such a manner that they become easily identifiable to other lawyers and court personnel. Nor do these firms provide an organizational hierarchy or internal labor market that provides advancement and prestige to help make up for lost professional status. If franchise law firm lawyers maintain any prestige, it is based upon the myth that they are in the same position as lawyers with independent practices. In fact, the ideology of the small business owner provides lawyers with their strongest justification for joining franchise law firm practices.

However, most lawyers join franchise law firms because they find their choices severely limited in an overcrowded labor market. This is especially true of the inexperienced law school graduates who populate the franchise law firm's lowest ranks as staff attorneys. They turn to these firms only after weeks of unsuccessful job searches. The burden of student loans forces young lawyers to accept employment with firms that, because they advertise on television, will not help to build positive reputations within their legal communities. They then become subject to production systems that require little legal skill, training or experience. Nonetheless, they hope to eventually leave the franchise law firm to open their own legal practices. The small-business ideology of their managing attorneys suggests that such a goal is reasonable, if not readily obtainable.

The juxtaposition of professional norms and the economic realities of professional practice have long been a concern of both the legal profession (Solomon 1992) and the literature on the professions (see, e.g., Abbott 1988; Abel 1989, 1988a, 1988b, 1981; Freidson 1994, 1986; Larson 1977; Parsons 1954). The bar's actions have been confined to an almost cyclical fretting about the public's lack of respect for lawyers and the commercialization of legal practices. With few exceptions, the professions literature argues that economic markets are not as important as professional norms and knowledge (Abbott 1988; Parsons 1954), or that the professions monopolize markets in a manner that empowers practitioners both within organizations and in client relationships (Abel 1989, 1988a, 1988b; Freidson 1994, 1986; Larson 1977). These theories provide competing perspectives about how the professions have come to be treated differently from other occupations by society and what such differential treatment means for professional workers and their clients. For example, functionalist theory treats professions as a particular form of social organization with normative features (Nelson and Trubek 1992). Professional organization is characterized as based on esoteric knowledge which provides a conceptual separation from other types of businesses (Parsons 1954, p. 38). In this view, professions are different from other occupations because the professional is interested in performing a useful service *rather than making a profit* (Parsons 1954, p. 35). This service orientation and production of specialized knowledge means that professional workers, unlike other occupations, must have autonomy and independence (Carr-Saunders and Wilson 1933).

In contrast to functionalism, Freidson (1970, p. xvii) argues that "it is useful to think of a profession as an occupation which has assumed a dominant position in a division of labor, so that it gains control over the determination of the substance of its own work." In a similar vein, Larson (1977) and others who follow the monopoly approach (Abel 1989, 1988a, 1988b; Starr 1982) argue that professions successfully monopolize markets for esoteric knowledge. The result of this process is a decline of competition among practitioners, increasing status and a powerful dominance over clients and other lay people who know little about expert knowledge. Freidson has largely been concerned with how professional dominance of the division of labor affects the relationship between professionals and clients. The monopoly perspective focuses on attempts by professionals to develop, maintain and expand markets for services. Both professional dominance and monopoly approaches treat professions as relatively closed institutions. Achieving social closure means that internal professional actions and characteristics are viewed as more important than external social factors when considering professional development and change.

Abbott (1988) has developed a complex ecological theory of a system of professions which is characterized by competition among professional groups and occupations aspiring to professional status. Abbott argues that professions and other occupations compete in an essentially closed social system for the resources to define and control a limited number of esoteric knowledge jurisdictions. Equilibrating forces are at work at the center of the system, providing the stability that established professions are supposed to enjoy.

Abbott's ecological theory, functionalism, professional dominance and monopoly theories all treat professions as closed institutions or social systems. The result is a tendency for the professions literature to ignore social factors that are considered external to professional institutions. This is particularly true of economic markets, since each theory treats professions as protected from both external and internal market competition—through professional norms, market monopolies or closed social systems that are devoid of capitalist market influences. These approaches to the professions have provided many illuminating insights. Nonetheless, by excluding market forces from their analyses, theories of the professions have excluded an important element of the environment in which professionals interact with clients, their employers and the larger society (see also Nelson 1988).

The rise of franchise law firms provides a striking example of how the legal profession and its practitioners have become subject to economic market forces over the past 30 years. However, the effects of market competition have not been felt equally by all practitioners. Corporate lawyers have seen their status and wealth increase as large law firms have competed to hire the best and brightest law school graduates to serve businesses willing to pay a premium for specialized services tailored to their needs (Nelson 1988; Galanter and Palay 1992). Personal services lawyers, on the other hand, have become increasingly impoverished, in both wealth and professional status, as more and more lawyers have entered this segment of the profession. Competition here is not between the best and the brightest lawyers, but about providing the lowest cost divorces, personal bankruptcy filings, residential real estate closings and name changes. Franchise law firms have developed in the personal services sector of the legal marketplace at a time when competition has become focused on the price of services rather than the quality of services. In such an environment all providers of legal services are forced to become more efficient. Nonetheless, franchise law firms succeed because they mass produce and mass market basic legal services to individuals more efficiently than other providers of those same services. To fully understand how franchise law firms have innovated in the production and marketing of legal services, it is first necessary to examine the structure of the legal profession. Franchise law firms are the result of a historical process that has divided the legal profession into upper-level and lower-level market segments with different sets of skills and opportunities.

LAW: TWO PROFESSIONS IN ONE PACKAGE

Stratification among legal practitioners was documented as early as the 1921 Reed Report. In this report on legal education, conducted for the American Bar Association, Reed suggests that law be formally divided into two professions based on divisions already present in the profession. One bar, comprised of lawyers trained at expensive, full-time law schools, would serve the needs of business; a separate bar of lawyers, trained at night law schools, would include probate, criminal, and trial practices (Reed 1921; see Auerbach 1976, pp. 110–113 for a discussion).

Although Reed's proposals were never adopted, his observation that the legal profession is stratified is echoed throughout the literature on the legal profession. Auerbach (1976) argues that there has been one main cleavage that characterizes the legal profession throughout its history. That cleavage is between elite, white Protestant lawyers and status-seeking, working-class ethnic and racial minorities. Auerbach argues that white elite lawyers conspired to use bar associations, training requirements, licensing standards and exclusion from prestigious law firms to construct barriers to entering the profession. Where minorities have entered the profession, Auerbach argues, they have been relegated to low-income, low-status positions.

Carlin (1994) concluded his classic study of solo-practicing attorneys in Chicago with the observation that the bar is split between high-status attorneys who work at large corporate law firms and marginalized sole-practicing lawyers.

One fact stands out clearly from this study of Chicago lawyers: the lawyer practicing by himself is generally at the bottom of the status ladder of the metropolitan bar. Although once held in the highest esteem as the model of a free, independent professional, today the individual practitioner of law, like the general practitioner in medicine, is most likely to be found at the margin of his profession, enjoying little freedom in choice of clients, type of work, or conditions of practice. (p. 207)

Like Auerbach, Carlin found that ethnic minorities were marginalized as independent practitioners while WASPs dominated the corporate law firm.

Heinz and Laumann (1982) conducted an extensive survey of the social structure of the Chicago bar. They found it to be so divided by specialty, type of practice, ethnicity and politics that they concluded the legal profession could be broken down into many different professions. Nevertheless, Heinz and Laumann find that one major cleavage divides Chicago lawyers, namely, the clients one serves—personal clients or large organizations (e.g., individuals versus corporations, labor unions and government). Each area of legal practice is so distinct that Heinz and Laumann call them "hemispheres" (1982, p. 319). The authors found that only 14 percent of their 699 respondents reported doing substantial work for both corporations *and* individuals or small businesses (1982, p. 55). "Most lawyers reside exclusively in one hemisphere or the other and seldom, if ever, cross the equator" (Heinz and Laumann 1982, p. 319).

Not only are the two hemispheres of the legal profession relatively separate, the lawyers working in each are also quite distinct. For example, Heinz and Laumann found 36 percent of lawyers working in the field of corporate securities to be Protestant, 9 percent Catholic, and 14 percent Jewish. In contrast, none of the divorce lawyers in their sample were Protestant, but 26 percent were Catholic and 56 percent were Jewish. Forty-five percent of securities lawyers attended elite law schools, while only 11 percent of divorce lawyers attended elite schools. Sixty-one percent of divorce lawyers reported working as solo practitioners, while 77 percent of securities lawyers reported working in law firms of more than 30 lawyers (1982, p. 65). The research evidence clearly supports the thesis that the legal profession is divided into two almost totally separate markets for services.

The cleavage between lawyers working in the personal services sector and those serving large organizations goes beyond differences in the social characteristics of the lawyers. Although the number of lawyers has more than tripled since the 1960s[1] and the legal profession has become a fast growing industry,[2] growth across the profession has been quite unequal. Feeding the growth of the legal industry has been an emphasis on corporate law. From 1967 to 1982 business legal services grew at almost twice the rate of personal legal services (Sander and Williams 1989, pp. 440–441). The demand for lawyers at large law firms serving corporate clients has sent associate salaries skyrocketing. Sander and Williams (1989, p. 474) report that at the nation's "elite" law firms, associate salaries have risen from an average of $14,000 in 1967 to over $80,000 in 1987. Partner incomes at the same firms have also increased—from an average of $79,000 in 1967 to $335,000 in 1988.

But in contrast to the large elite law firms, small-firm lawyers and solo practitioners have not fared well. Partner incomes at the "non-elite" law firms which tend to serve personal clients declined by at least 10 percent between the 1970s and 1980s. In 1986 starting salaries of associates at small law firms (two to eight attorneys) averaged only $25,000 (Sander and Williams 1989, p. 474). From the early 1970s to 1985 the incomes of sole-practicing

attorneys declined by 30 percent. By 1985 the average income of
solo practitioners was still less than $25,000 (Sander and Williams
1989, p. 475). Sander and Williams (1989, pp. 468–469) suggest
that this decline in incomes is closely related to a rapid rise in the
number of solo practitioners. Indeed, the number of sole-practicing
lawyers increased 34 percent from 1980 to 1988 (Curran and
Carson 1991, p. 6). Individual practitioners are the largest segment
of the legal profession, comprising almost a third of all practicing lawyers and 46 percent of lawyers in private practice (Curran
and Carson 1991, p. 6; Sander and Williams 1989, pp. 468–
469). Given the increasing numbers of solo practitioners and the
declining rate of growth of the personal legal services market, unemployment and underemployment have become common occur-
rences among the lawyers who serve individual clients and small
businesses (see also Nelson and Trubek 1992). Thus, competition
for personal legal services clients is intensifying as the number of
lawyers increases faster than the market is able to grow.[3]

PERSONAL LEGAL SERVICES

As the above discussion suggests, each of the two legal markets
that characterize the legal profession is distinct and has its own
dynamics. While the workplace practices of the corporate sector of
the profession are well-known (see Galanter and Palay 1992; Nelson 1988; Poor 1994; Smigel 1969; Spangler 1986), there are few
studies of lawyers in metropolitan personal services markets (but
see Carlin 1994, 1966; and Seron 1996, 1993). However, there are
a number of studies of lawyers in related practice contexts. These
include the social structure of attorneys in rural settings (Landon
1990), legal aid attorneys (Katz 1982; Spangler 1986), public de-
fenders (McIntyre 1987), general practice attorneys (Cain 1983),
divorce lawyers (Jacob 1990; O'Gorman 1963; Sarat and Felstiner
1995, 1986), personal injury attorneys (Rosenthal 1974) and consumer protection lawyers (Macaulay 1979).

The picture of legal practice painted by this literature is dis-
heartening, especially for individual practitioners. As discussed
above, lawyers in the personal services sector of the profession are
likely to have attended law schools of moderate to low prestige
and earn modest livings. Carlin described the typical individual

practitioner as a "self-made man," the son of "an immigrant from Eastern Europe with little or no formal education [who] was in most cases the proprietor of a small business" (1994, p. 3). The desire to escape from the ghetto led the attorneys to attend local law schools at night to obtain professional degrees.

Clients are gained by referrals from other clients, attorneys and personal networks (Carlin 1994, pp. 123–141; Ladinsky 1976; Landon 1990, pp. 127–133; Jacob 1990). Many clients are "one-shotters" and cannot be counted on to return to the lawyer on a regular basis (Galanter 1974). Carlin's (1994, pp. 124–130) lawyers believed that to be successful practitioners they needed to develop client bases beyond family and friends by participating in ethno-religious or civic organizations. However, Carlin found no relationship between organizational participation and economic or professional success.

Word-of-mouth referrals and competition for clients means lawyers in the personal client hemisphere may be tempted into unethical behavior. For example, Carlin (1994, p. 148) found that many sole practitioners paid kickbacks to "brokers" who sent them clients on a regular basis (also see Carlin 1966). Rosenthal (1976) describes plaintiff's personal injury lawyers who counsel clients to accept settlements that maximize the lawyer's earnings at the expense of the client's award. And before the advent of no-fault divorce laws, attorneys routinely created sham adultery complaints to facilitate their clients' cases (O'Gorman 1963).

The work of personal services lawyers is largely routine and is seldom path-breaking. Carlin (1994) divided the work of solo practitioners in Chicago into upper-level and lower-level categories to distinguish successful lawyers from their less successful counterparts. Lower-level attorneys tend to be grounded in a particular neighborhood where they serve working-class individuals and owners of small businesses by acting as service brokers. The work of these lawyers consisted of bringing the client into contact with other professionals, businesses or governmental agencies (e.g., another lawyer, real estate or insurance agents, banks, etc.) (Carlin 1994, pp. 114–115).

Upper-level attorneys, on the other hand, have moved beyond a particular neighborhood. Many have ongoing ventures with business or real estate clients (also see Landon 1990). Nonetheless,

Carlin found the work of all individual practitioners to be so routine that they are "rarely called upon to exercise a high level of professional skill" (1994, p. 207). Furthermore, Carlin reports that upper-level personal injury, divorce and tax lawyers are able to develop "the mass production character of their practice" because they "are somewhat less frequently called upon to perform high-level technical skills than are upper-level real estate [commercial transactions] and business-corporate lawyers" (1994, p. 115).

Heinz and Laumann's (1982) survey of the Chicago bar suggests that Carlin's findings may be applicable to a large segment of personal services practitioners. Only 42 percent of the lawyers in their "personal plight" category reported that their work was too complex for lay people to understand and complete. In contrast, 62 percent of the lawyers in the "large corporate" category believe their work is too complex for lay people to understand. Even more striking, 72 percent of securities lawyers report their work is so highly specialized that they can concentrate in only that one area of law. But only 23 percent of divorce lawyers, 26 percent of probate lawyers and 36 percent of all lawyers in the personal plight category report their work to be highly specialized (1982, pp. 65, 70).

CONSTANTS AND CHANGE IN PERSONAL LEGAL SERVICES

I interviewed a randomly drawn sample of 35 individual-practicing and small-firm lawyers in the Chicago metropolitan area, using the interview schedule from Carlin's 1962 study (reissued in 1994; see the appendix for research methods). With few exceptions, the social characteristics of my sample are quite similar to Carlin's sample of Chicago solo practitioners. Yet there are subtle changes in how personal services lawyers organize their work to compete in the current market for services. The typical lawyer in my sample is a second or third generation descendent of European background (primarily Irish, German, Italian, or East European Jew) who was born and raised in Chicago or one of the suburbs surrounding Chicago. There are no African Americans, only one Hispanic and six women in my sample.

Fourteen percent of the respondents' fathers are members of a profession, 54 percent are proprietors of small businesses, 20 percent are white-collar workers, and 11 percent are blue-collar workers. The majority of the respondents' fathers are high school graduates (51 percent); 14 percent have four-year college degrees, 14 percent have graduate (professional) degrees, 11 percent did not finish high school and 11 percent did not finish grammar school.[4] All but two of the respondents in my sample attended local Chicago law schools—primarily John Marshal, IIT-Kent, Depaul University and Loyola University. None of the respondents in my sample attended the law schools of the University of Chicago, Northwestern University or the University of Illinois. Forty-six percent attended law school at night while also holding full-time jobs during the day.

Like Carlin's individual practitioners (see 1994, pp. 4–6), only a few of the lawyers in my sample intended to become attorneys when they started college. The majority of lawyers I interviewed turned to law after working in other, often non-professional, occupations for a period of time. They turned to law as the easiest route to what they thought would be a more lucrative or intellectually challenging career in the professions. Craig explains how he "fell" into law:

I'll tell you . . . it was a dead-end job that I was in and I knew I had to do something. I wasn't, couldn't get anything with my criminal justice major from college—that was another dead end. . . .

Megan chose law after deciding that becoming a doctor might take too long.

I originally was going to be a doctor, then I got married and had children, and so forth. So then later, as the children got raised, I looked for something . . . interesting, and so that's the way I went.

Despite their hopes for affluence and intellectual stimulation, a number of the attorneys I interviewed report supplementing their law practices with other types of work or retreating from the practice of law all together. For example, only one of the three people with law and accounting degrees I interviewed remains a practicing lawyer today (though all were practicing attorneys at the time of the interviews). Although all had hoped their legal careers would be more challenging and stimulating than accountancy, they found practicing law to provide an unstable income and have returned to careers in accounting. Another attorney described himself as "basically a real estate agent," while a fourth respondent gave up the practice of law to work in the office of a medical building.

Despite the overcrowded labor market, the attorneys in my sample shun newer techniques for gaining clients (see also Abel 1989; Seron 1996, 1993). None advertise on television and only one advertises in newspapers (though most do have listings, but not display advertisements, in the yellow pages of the telephone directory). None of the attorneys in my sample participate in prepaid legal services plans, and only a few participate in bar association referral services.[5] About a third of the attorneys I interviewed have experimented with at least one of these marketing techniques, but did not find them cost-effective. Malcolm's experience with a prepaid legal services plan is typical:

I remember somebody called me, a friend of mine from law school, and asked me if I was interested in doing one of these prepaid legal plans for him, being his contact in divorce work. I said, "sure, I'll try it." So, I did . . . I think I did three clients and it was such a waste. I mean, I don't know how people do it. I suppose if . . . see, my practice just doesn't lend itself to that, because I, mine isn't the, you know, 50 divorces in a day. You know, mine is holding hands and stroking people, and the people with prepaid legal services, they're the guys that can't afford to put in the personal time. So I just, I did three clients and it was such, it was such a loser on the money that I told him I wasn't interested. I could lose money on my own without taking his cases.

Other attorneys, such as Abe and Karen (respectively), also describe their experiences with bar association referral services and advertising as ineffective:

We found that the kinds of cases that you would get from [referral services] would be real marginal. . . . You know, the person with a 200-dollar personal injury claim who thought that he wanted to take it to the Supreme Court. You know, that kind of stuff is what the bar association does. [Referral service clients want] a lawyer that will fight for them all the way to the Supreme Court, because this guy, you know, damaged his car for $150 worth.

I have a couple of friends who manage realty offices that have conned me into . . . buying an ad in these books that they put out, you know, to new home buyers. They haven't gotten, those haven't gotten me a penny. I can really tell you that. Those have not gotten me a penny. . . . I don't think I've gotten one piece of business out of those.

Referrals from satisfied clients, other attorneys, or business acquaintances (real estate brokers, accountants, etc.) are still the preferred method of obtaining new clients. These practitioners describe their "business strategy" as trying to satisfy their clients. This is true regardless of the area of law the attorney may concentrate in. Compare the business strategies of two Chicago sole practitioners. The first concentrates in residential real estate; the second concentrates in incorporating small businesses:

Most of my contacts [are] real estate agents that I met at closings. I was able to get things done when there was a problem, and so then they began to refer [clients] to me. . . . [But] my constant strategy is doing a good job and don't rip them [clients] off. . . .

The principal way that . . . small practice, solo practitioners get business is from your other clients. People that you meet when you're in the business and they're impressed with how you do business. That's been my experience anyway.

Only the two plaintiff's personal injury lawyers in the sample report taking a more active role in obtaining new clients. Partners at plaintiff's personal injury firms such as Mark try to promote their expertise to other lawyers by publishing articles and giving lectures on particular areas of law:

I write a number of articles in the professional [journals] on specific topics that very few attorneys know anything about. For instance, I have these two large . . . asbestos-related cases and I have written an article on the law . . . in this area. It's pretty complex stuff. Most attorneys know nothing about it, so the article itself is kind of . . . a primer on asbestos law, you know? But that's one of the purposes—to help attorneys with stuff that's out there. . . . But its secondary purpose may be subliminal, or maybe it's obvious, that, you know, we are the people who handle those cases and [we have] pretty much cornered that market in this part of the country, okay? Now, in other areas we are doing the same thing, not as successfully—we haven't cornered the market—but I give lectures to groups of attorneys. One drew 300 attorneys last week. . . . So what happens? It increases business, it increases your professional standing. All that stuff is almost a normal end for that type of work.

Plaintiff's personal injury lawyers stand out with their more obvious marketing techniques that champion their "legal expertise" to gain client referrals. Personal injury work has become particularly competitive in recent years, with some attorneys advertising their services on radio and television. The organization of plaintiff's personal injury work also reflects this competitive environment and mirrors innovations at franchise law firms. Plaintiff's personal injury lawyers delegate virtually all tasks, except depositions and court appearances, to paralegals or secretaries.[6]

Most anything that can be [delegated] is. For instance, there are a lot of documents that are legal documents but they've been prepared many times before. So we'll often have someone else do all the preparations and we'll have an attorney read them before we file, but it saves a lot of time when someone else is doing all the preparation for you. We have paralegals. They didn't have paralegals when we first started. We probably have half a dozen paralegals right now. A number of secretaries, you know, we have over 10 now, are also paralegals and they can do these tremendous things, reducing the attorney's work.

Among the other attorneys I interviewed the tasks delegated to support staff differ, depending on the type of law being dealt with.[7] Attorneys specializing in residential real estate closings or wills and estate planning appear to have highly routinized practices. Real estate closings and simple wills often involve only minimal contact with clients. The work in these areas mostly involves filling out forms. With the advent of computerized word processing, the form work is easily delegated to secretaries or paralegals. Shawn, a sole practitioner who concentrates on residential real estate delegates

everything I can. She opens the files, she keeps contact with the realtors, you know? And in real estate practice she's got to spend a lot of time on the phone with lenders, realtors, other attorneys, clients, pulling all the pieces together so that you've got the title and the survey, and all the other documents ready. And the ideal for a real estate lawyer is to have somebody out there that's good enough that you can open the file with a client, hand it to the secretary and not look at it again until you go to the closing. That's the way to run a profitable real estate practice. . . . So she's right here, we work together.

While real estate work appears to be routine enough that attorneys delegate much of their work to secretaries, attorneys that perform estate planning tend to use paralegals. Karen, an attorney who is a former paralegal describes the paralegal's unacknowledged role in drafting wills and trusts while explaining what led her to become an attorney:

The firm I worked for . . . had an associate attorney working for them. Now, this fellow had been an attorney and had numerous jobs. . . . He was not a just out of school attorney. . . . I did all the paralegal work in the area of estate planning. He would come to me with information on clients. He'd say, "I want you to write a will or trust for this person." . . . And he'd hand me all the information and I would look at it and I would go to him and I'd say, "John, why are you doing this? Why would you not do it this way," you know? And, he'd say, "Good idea," and he'd pick up the phone before I could say another word and he'd dial his client and he'd say, you know, "Hey Jack, I've just been thinking [about] this and I'm thinking, you know, I think this is really the better route to go and here's why. . . ."

So, at any rate, I give him a lot of credit for my becoming a lawyer. One day I was talking to him and I was drafting [a trust] and I said to him, "Oh, by the way, do you want me to write a transmittal letter [about] . . . sending the drafts out to the client or do you want to write that?" And he looked at me and he said, "Well, what's the normal?" And I said, "Well, this attorney over here always has me write the transmittal letters and this attorney over here likes to write his own transmittal letters. So, I'm just asking which way you prefer?" And he said, "Oh, you write the letter, you write the letter." . . . I walked out of his office, got down the hall and I heard him shouting, "Karen, Karen." And I went back and he said to me, he said, "I want you to write the letter but it's to go out over my signature." And I said, "Absolutely." I said, "every one of those letters goes out over the attorney's signature." And he says to me, "Good, that's the way it ought to be. After all, you're only a paralegal!" And at that point I decided, if this jerk could get through law school, I could do it.

The divorce lawyers in my sample also report delegating most of their drafting tasks to secretaries. The routine nature of many divorce complaints, judgments for dissolution and letters to clients allows secretaries to "spit them out from examples already on the computer." Divorce lawyers claim that giving writing and drafting tasks to secretaries allows them more time to spend with clients. Like Malcolm, the attorney who found that his divorce practice is not compatible with prepaid legal services plans, these lawyers report that "holding hands and stroking people" is an important part of helping clients through painful divorces and separations. As will be shown, a major difference between the traditional personal services lawyer and franchise law firms is the amount of time lawyers spend with clients to explain the law, offer options and counsel the outraged or hurting to feel better (see Chapter 4). The time required for these services is not available to lawyers at franchise law firms. Not all individual and small-firm lawyers delegate as much of their work to secretaries or paralegals as personal injury, real estate, estate planning and divorce lawyers appear to. Business-corporate, patent-trademark and criminal defense attorneys delegate only the typing of dictation or pre-drafted documents to their secretaries. In fact, the criminal defense lawyer in my sample does not employ a secretary at all. The bulk of his day is spent with his clients in court. An old, portable typewriter is sufficient for the small amount of drafting and writing necessary in his legal practice.

Significantly, business-corporate and patent-trademark lawyers have corporate, rather than personal services clients. Although they describe their clients as small corporations and businesses, they consider the work complex enough that it cannot be given to support staff to complete. For example, the patent-trademark attorney refers to patent work as "just, basically, creative writing" and a business-corporate lawyer reports that the most important thing his secretary does is "to keep a central diary system for all things that are in litigation" so that court dates are not missed.

The data I have presented in this section generally support the findings of Carlin (1994) and Heinz and Laumann (1982). Lawyers offering personal legal services appear to be from modest social backgrounds, attend local law schools and perform more routine services for individual clients than is the case for lawyers serving even small corporations. The lawyers I describe most closely resemble Carlin's upper-level practitioners where "the mass production character of their practice allows them to standardize most technical aspects of their work" (1994, p. 115). But where Carlin had only personal injury, tax and divorce work in this category, I now add real estate and estate planning. However, this does not mean that real estate closings or constructing wills have become less complex. On the contrary, these services were previously considered so routine that they were regularly performed by non-lawyers (real estate brokers, banks, etc.) (see Carlin 1994, pp. 52–62, 101–105).

What I did not find is evidence of lower-level practitioners who act primarily as brokers or intermediaries rather than legal services providers (see Carlin 1994, p. 114). Although more research is necessary, it seems likely that Carlin's lower-level practitioner has been displaced by the increasing competition among neighborhood lawyers and new providers of legal services in metropolitan areas. Legal aid, legal clinics, prepaid legal services plans and franchise law firms are filling the void where lower-level attorneys once practiced. The new providers offer services to consumers who may be poor or have middle-level incomes and some small businesses.

FRANCHISE LAW FIRM LAWYERS

Support for the thesis that new providers are displacing lower-level legal practitioners can be found by examining the social characteristics of franchise law firm lawyers. The profile of franchise law firm lawyers is strikingly similar to that of solo and small-firm attorneys. Most of the attorneys in my nationwide sample of franchise law firm lawyers (see appendix) are the grandchildren or great-grandchildren of immigrants from Italy, Ireland, Germany, Russia or Poland. Almost 20 percent of the attorneys are Jewish and only 8 percent are WASP. There are three Hispanics, one African American, and eight women in my sample.

Forty-two percent of the respondents' fathers are proprietors of small businesses, 27 percent are white-collar workers, 16 percent are blue-collar workers and 15 percent are members of a profession. Ten percent of the respondents' fathers have law degrees, 15 percent have graduate (master's) degrees, 15 percent have four-year college degrees, 11 percent attended two years of college, 26 percent are high school graduates and 24 percent completed only grammar school.

All but three of the attorneys employed by franchise law firms attended local law schools rather than the more prestigious, nationally known law schools. Most of these lawyers report graduating in the middle to top one-third of their law school classes. About 21 percent of franchise attorneys report attending law school at night.

Like other personal services lawyers, almost half of the franchise law firm attorneys considered or tried other occupations before choosing law. John and Sam (respectively) offer typical examples:

When I was in college I wanted to be a child psychiatrist and a playwright. And after I did [a] year's worth of graduate-type courses . . . my father said, "I'll keep supporting you but it's got to be a degree more worthwhile than a Ph.D. in English." So, since I don't like the sight of blood, I figured, well, law school is probably less bloody than medical school.

I didn't want to be a lawyer all my life, I just evolved into deciding that being a lawyer would be better than retiring from the police department and winding up being a bank guard for the rest of my life.

Lawyers employed by franchise law firms come from similar social backgrounds, have similar law school experiences and have similar aspirations to other personal services lawyers. However, if franchise law firms and other new providers of legal services are filling the gap where lower-level attorneys once practiced, they are doing so in a radically different way. Instead of providing a conduit between clients and other service providers, franchise law firms offer consumers a limited set of mass-produced services.

LEGAL AID, LEGAL CLINICS AND FRANCHISE LAW FIRMS

Legal clinics and franchise law firms compete with other lawyers for clients by offering personal services at competitive, flat fees instead of charging hourly rates.[8] It is no accident that franchise law firms and legal clinics share this trait. Most franchise firms began as legal clinics. Legal clinics were thought of as inheriting and extending the legal services movement begun by legal assistance attorneys (see Katz 1982, for an examination of the legal services movement). Where legal aid offices serve the poor and indigent, legal clinics were to increase access to legal services for middle-income people. Taking their cue from legal aid, legal clinics were supposed to be "high volume, streamlined, efficient, and impersonal" but profitable operations (American Bar Association 1982, p. 6). Legal clinics defined a "new" market of legal services patrons to be served at retail-style outlets.[9]

However, American Bar Association (1990, 1982) studies conclude that legal clinics are not particularly high volume, efficient, impersonal, or profitable. The studies suggest there is little difference between legal clinics and other small law practices. Legal clinics simply appear to be small law offices owned by a single lawyer. In fact, by the 1980s solo and small-firm practitioners were employing the few innovations legal clinics were known for (such as setting flat fees for routine services like personal bankruptcy, uncontested divorce and wills, and running advertisements in the yellow pages). Plagued by low profits, legal clinics seem to be disappearing from the personal legal services landscape (American Bar Association 1990).

While most legal clinics have apparently failed to live up to expectations, some successfully developed into franchise law firms. Franchise law firms have become the high-volume, streamlined, and efficient operations envisioned for legal clinics. Legal clinics (and prepaid legal services plans) helped to revolutionize the *sale* of personal legal services by popularizing flat fees. However, franchise law firms have developed efficient *production* and marketing systems that allow branch offices to profitably serve a high volume of clients on a flat fee basis. To do so they have developed production systems that emphasize routine legal services and require minimal legal counseling.

Franchise law firms exist at both regional and national levels. The largest of the national firms boasts 150 offices employing 300–400 attorneys who serve an estimated 175,000 clients annually.[10] These firms have pioneered techniques of law firm expansion that circumvent American Bar Association (ABA) rules prohibiting non-lawyers from owning law firms. Many franchise law firms have spun off independent management companies to provide equipment and services to the law firm. The management companies, not bound by ABA rules governing law firm ownership, seek investments for capital improvement and expansion of the law firm. Before the innovation of independent management companies, law firms were forced to expand based on lawyer investment and law firm earnings. Non-lawyer investments have allowed some firms to explode from five or ten offices to more than 100 offices in a few years.

While most individual and small-firm practicing lawyers shun advertising as expensive and ineffective, franchise law firms embrace television advertising. Indeed, franchise law firms pioneered advertising by lawyers on television after the U.S. Supreme Court legalized attorney advertising in 1977.[11] Television advertising sets franchise law firms apart from most other lawyers. Even legal clinics, which pioneered the format of offering routine legal services at reduced, fixed fees, advertise very little (American Bar Association 1990, p. 25).

With television advertising, franchise law firms address a large potential market of clients who might otherwise have no contact with lawyers. Franchise law firms use television advertising to create a market niche of clients that may not be connected to other lawyers through family and friends. Although franchise law firms compete with other lawyers for new clients, they also target the population of potential clients who rarely or never consult lawyers when legal problems arise. This population may be as large as two-thirds of all adult U.S. citizens (Curran 1977).

Advertising is but one response to the highly competitive personal legal services market. In an environment where both jobs and clients are scarce it is likely that professionals will seek to lower overhead costs and increase productivity, as well as seek new clients and differentiate themselves from competitors. The advent of inexpensive, personal computers allows for the streamlining of routine writing and drafting tasks for virtually all lawyers. Specialization and the use of computers undoubtedly makes it easier for professionals to delegate tasks to support staff who have little or no formal legal training (Haug 1977). Franchise law firms use computers and specialization in addition to television advertising to reorganize the sale, production and delivery of personal legal services in a manner that takes advantage of the overcrowded labor market for lawyers.

By standardizing each service the franchise firm gains a number of competitive advantages. First, standardization allows branch office staffs to service clients efficiently by assigning many legal decision-making and production tasks to secretaries. At franchise law firms secretaries take over responsibility for determining the types of legal problems clients have and producing the letters and documents necessary for dealing with the problems. The main role of lawyers is to sell clients one of the services that the firm offers. Because all services are offered in only one format, attorneys are forced to offer clients relatively standard solutions based on *prepackaged* production systems. The attorney who informs a client that the firm's simple will "has everything you'll ever need" has only that one will available within the firm's production system. The only choices are to sell the services that are available or sell no services at all. Problems that do not fit the standardized solutions, or clients who are hard to deal with, are usually turned away to avoid taxing efficiency and profits.[12]

A second competitive benefit of franchise law firms stems from the prepackaging of legal solutions for easy access by lawyers and secretaries. The productivity gains brought about by delegating legal decision-making tasks to secretaries and limiting lawyer autonomy allows large numbers of clients to be processed through branch offices on a regular basis. Franchise law firms develop high-volume production systems which make it feasible to employ television advertising to attract new clients. Television advertising differentiates franchise firms in a competitive market and helps to consistently supply branch offices with clients. The success of television advertising allows attorneys to have little concern for repeat business and helps to insulate branch offices from direct price competition with other lawyers.

Television advertising and standardized production systems help franchise law firms to develop economies of scale that make offering legal services at competitive fees (often a flat rate for each service) profitable. However, the profit margin on each case is small. Thus incentive systems at franchise law firms emphasize productivity by making each office or each lawyer a profit center with compensation tied to sales. Attorneys gain an interest in selling the services that can be processed quickly and efficiently because that is how profits—and higher compensation—are generated.

A third benefit of prepackaging law is that standardized production allows franchise law firms to take advantage of the buyer's market for lawyers. Inexperienced lawyers who find they are unable to secure other employment are willing to work for relatively low pay to gain experience and steady work. Of the attorneys with work experience prior to joining a franchise law firm, many report earning less than $25,000 a year and some report annual incomes as low as $12,000. These attorneys sought employment at franchise law firms as a shield from the uncertainties of working in small partnerships or as solo practitioners when no other work is available. Sam, who joined a franchise law firm after seven years as a sole practitioner, explains that

> there was one year I earned something like $170,000 in gross [income, but] because I had been so far in the hole for the three previous years I wound up paying taxes that year on about $3,000 of net [profit]. It wasn't really great. . . . That's what I call . . . fighting the bear. You fight the bear for seven or eight years out there and this job doesn't look all that bad. No job looks all that bad.

The prepackaging of personal legal services also makes it possible for attorneys with little experience to immediately begin working with little supervision. Standardized production techniques make experts unnecessary because decision-making discretion is limited, as a staff attorney explains, to "mak[ing] a sale or tell[ing] [clients] that we can't help them." When attorneys become too frustrated with their limited range of options, experiences and the low pay, the production system and market forces make replacing them quick, easy and inexpensive.

Just as McDonald's uses computers and other technology to reorganize restaurant kitchen work into a fast-paced production line (Garson 1988, pp. 17–39), these firms reorganize personal legal services work in a similar fashion. This production line approach provides predictability and control as well as efficiency in the work process and client services (Garson 1988; Ritzer 1996, p. 25). The trade-off for professionals is that they become salespeople in a production system that seeks and creates workers who are motivated almost solely by material wealth and are alienated from their clients. In many cases, alienation is increased by firm organization and incentive systems that encourage competition among coworkers but provide no reward for achieving success. In the remainder of this book I provide a detailed ethnography of two of the nation's largest franchise law firms, Arthur & Nelson and Beck & Daniels. My analysis shows the pervasive control involved and the contradictory nature of mass producing and mass marketing legal advice and services to consumers.

NOTES

1. The number of lawyers and judges in the United States has increased from 218,000 in 1960 to 757,000 in 1988. From the mid-1970s through the early 1980s the number of lawyers grew by almost 25,000 people a year. Since 1970 the legal profession has grown three times as fast as the professions in general, and twice as fast as doctors (Sander and Williams 1989, pp. 432–433).

2. In the early 1960s there were only 38 law firms with 50 or more lawyers in the United States (Smigel 1969; Galanter and Palay 1992). But by 1988 the number of firms with 51 or more lawyers had ballooned to 639 (Curran and Carson 1991, p. 12; see also Galanter and Palay 1992). Sander and Williams (1989, p. 435) estimate that "the total economic scale of the [legal services] industry by 1987 was probably more than $80 billion."

3. The 1990–1992 recession only added to this competition. Pashigian (1978) has shown that earnings in the personal legal services market are closely tied to upswings and downturns of the economy.

4. In comparison, Carlin's respondents' fathers were 63 percent proprietors, 19 percent white-collar, 12 percent blue-collar, and 6 percent professional. But while the majority of respondents in my sample report that their fathers have at least finished high school, Carlin found that 85 percent of his respondents' fathers had no education beyond grammar school (1994, p. 25).

5. In a nationwide survey Reidinger (1987) found that only 25 percent of lawyers advertise. Among those who do advertise, 86 percent use the telephone directory yellow pages, 12 percent use newspapers, 9 percent distribute leaflets, 8 percent advertise in magazines or journals, 3 percent advertise on the radio, 3 percent use television and 1 percent use billboards.

6. The issue of who actually performs legal tasks, attorneys or support staff, was not investigated by Carlin (1994, 1966). At the time of his studies paralegals were not highly utilized by lawyers. Nonetheless, Carlin (1994, p. 115) did note that the specialization of personal injury, divorce and tax lawyers rests on their business-getting abilities, not their technical skills. I use the delegation of tasks in professional offices as a measure of the routine nature of the work. Delegation of legal tasks to support staff is being utilized as a strategy to allow lawyers to increase productivity. Delegation of legal work to support staff is an integral part of the organization of work at franchise law firms.

7. Lawyers who report spending at least 30 percent of their time working in a particular area of law are considered specialized. My use of the 30 percent cut-off for specialization follows Carlin (1994). Heinz and Laumann (1982) use a 25 percent cut-off for determining specializations in their study of the Chicago bar. If I use the 25 percent cut-off there are no general practitioners in my sample.

Using the 30 percent cut-off, my sample has specializations as follows: Nine attorneys in the sample specialize in residential real estate; five specialize in wills, estate planning and probate; five specialize in business-corporate law; four specialize in divorce; one each specialize in criminal defense, plaintiffs personal injury and patent-trademark law. Five of the attorneys listed above have two specializations. Four of these five attorneys are real estate specialists who also have a significant number of business-corporate clients. In addition, the solo-practicing personal injury attorney also has a thriving divorce practice. Four attorneys in my sample may be considered general practitioners.

8. Hourly fee rates are not totally unknown at legal clinics or franchise law firms. Hourly fee rates may be invoked for the occasional extraordinary case at legal clinics or to discourage a difficult client from buying services at franchise law firms.

9. The personal legal services market has recently experienced an explosion of innovative "new providers" (Seron 1992). New providers include prepaid legal services plans in addition to legal aid, legal clinics and franchise law firms. Prepaid legal services plans construct a network of attorneys who agree to service the problems of clients who join the plan at reduced fees. Plan members agree to contribute monthly, quarterly or yearly membership fees to the networking organization for the privilege of having attorneys who offer free or reduced fee services "on retainer." While legal aid offices, legal clinics and franchise law firms all hire attorneys to work in their offices, legal services plans usually provide a marketing service for independent attorneys.

10. During their peak in the mid-1980s some franchise law firms had 300 local offices and employed as many as 600 attorneys.

11. *Bates & O'Steen v. Arizona State Bar* (1977).

12. Less scrupulous attorneys may attempt to sell clients standardized services that are not appropriate for their legal needs by redefining the issue. Although it is not clear how often this happens, good attorneys at franchise law firms are defined as those who can sell services to clients under any circumstances (see Chapter 3).

2

The Organization of Mass Production Law

Concepts such as franchising and mass production conjure up images of young (or now increasingly elderly) workers occupying positions which require little more than a warm body. Garson (1988, p. 20) quotes a young McDonald's employee to show the bleak work environment:

Don't worry, you don't have to understand. You follow the beepers, you follow the buzzers and you turn your meat as fast as you can. It's like I told you, to work at McDonald's you don't need a face, you don't need a brain. You need to have two hands and two legs and move 'em as fast as you can. That's the whole system. I wouldn't go back there again for anything.

Clearly, we do not have the same image in mind when we speak of attorneys. Even the most exploited attorneys, offering the most basic of services, acquire a level of knowledge and skill far superior to the unskilled worker. Therefore, it is necessary to define what is meant when the concepts of mass production and franchises are applied to the work of lawyers. Franchise law firms can be best understood as part of a process in American society Ritzer (1996) has called "McDonaldization." McDonaldization combines the principles of franchises, bureaucracies, scientific management and assembly lines to achieve a maximum level of rationalization in the creation and delivery of products and services. Within the context of law this means organizing the law firm and legal work to minimize the efforts of lawyers as experts and put more responsibility into the hands of support staff. In this chapter I discuss how franchise law firms have developed rational organizations that make the delivery of legal services efficient.

THE BASIC MODEL

Franchise law firms are chains of local law offices located in shopping malls, strip malls or other retail business districts. Despite my calling these firms "franchises," not all law firms which fit this model are truly franchised. Beck & Daniels currently requires that attorneys buy into the firm and pay royalties on their earnings. Arthur & Nelson offices remain entirely owned by its founding partners. Indeed, Beck & Daniels' transformation to the franchise format happened during the course of this study. Previous to re-organizing the firm, Beck & Daniels' structure was similar to traditional bureaucracies found in many corporations. I have chosen to call these firms "franchises" for a number of reasons. First, despite issues of ownership, Arthur & Nelson and Beck & Daniels share a number of "McDonaldized" qualities with modern franchises. For example, only a limited "menu" of services is offered and each service that is offered has been standardized. This standardization makes the same services obtained at any local or branch office quite similar. In addition, as we shall see, each local office employee has a specific and limited set of roles and responsibilities. Second, Arthur & Nelson and Beck & Daniels have been moving toward "McDonaldized" (or highly rationalized) organizational structures, the end result of which appears to be franchise-like (where attorneys are subjected to centralized control over the work they perform). And finally, throughout the course of the study, many office managers and employees referred to the firms as "franchises," suggesting that the concept serves as a commonly accepted description of branch office manager and employee experiences.

The typical branch office includes a managing attorney (who may also be an owner), one or more staff attorneys and a number of secretaries. Arthur & Nelson offices may be as small as a managing attorney and one secretary, with no staff attorneys, while Beck & Daniels offices usually include at least one staff attorney and two secretaries under the managing attorney. Between the branch offices and each firm's founding partners are two or three levels of management, including district, regional and, at Beck & Daniels, national managers. However, in the 1990s the trend at both firms has been to subject local office managing attorneys to less direct supervision and to cut the middle management ranks where possible. Thus, Arthur & Nelson rewards successful managing attorneys by promoting them to managing partners. The only difference between managing attorney and managing partner positions is the level of supervision. Managing partners report directly to the founding partners, bypassing middle management. Local partners at Beck & Daniels (managing attorneys who buy into the firm) are assessed monthly based on revenue generated, but have little supervision of day-to-day affairs.

POSITIONS AND ROLES

Managing Attorneys

Managing attorneys are contracted by the firms to operate each local or branch office. Experienced attorneys may be hired directly into managing attorney positions or staff attorneys may be promoted to fill such positions. Arthur & Nelson provides a minimal training session for the managing attorney position. During a two- to five-day orientation, managing attorneys are introduced to the firm's administrative forms and office procedures.

Beck & Daniels' policy is to hire even experienced attorneys as staff attorneys for a period of one month to one year to introduce them to the firm's procedures and production system. For example, Beck & Daniels managing attorneys must learn how to use the firm's "operation manual" which details everything from the responsibilities of each branch office employee, the hours each office must be open and how accounting and paperwork is to be handled, to what types of legal cases an attorney may work on, how a client should be treated, how to organize case files (including where staples are to be placed in file folders) and the number of times a telephone may ring before it must be answered. Firm management often presents such procedures as a road map to success. For example, a Beck & Daniels national manager explains that

attorneys are often bad businessmen, so we do everything for them. We tell them what to do, when to do it and how to do it. Our system frees them to just practice law and serve the client. If they can do that, they can make money for us.

Some managing attorneys, such as Frank, accept the view of management that the rigid procedures in the operations manual ensure success:

We've got a huge operations manual that standardizes operations here and [at] every other Beck & Daniels office. . . . To give you an example, for accounting there are procedures for handling the receipt of fees and costs . . . that sort of thing. It's the same here as with any Beck & Daniels office. There is no guesswork involved. There aren't 50 million ways to do things. That makes it easy. Office functions, for example, you know what our mission is, what our goal is in terms of client satisfaction, in terms of revenues, in terms of getting the work done, in terms of hiring legal assistants or attorneys—what to look for. All that is pretty much standardized. They tell us this is what we should look for, this is what we should expect, this is how it should be handled. And, as I said, it makes it very easy because if you follow the instructions, if you only deviate within accepted limits, then all this has been worked out for us, all this has been tested, and all this has been successful here and elsewhere. If we utilize it, then it makes our job a lot easier.

Other attorneys, however, are less enthusiastic. Sam's comments are typical.

We have very definitive operating procedures. We have an extremely complicated office manual that outlines almost everything that you might want to know about how to do—including how to order a light bulb when it burns out in your office. So we have procedures on how to do everything.

They are pretty uniform and they are right here for anyone who wants to see them.

Managing attorneys earn a percentage of their office's profit as compensation. Arthur & Nelson takes a 35–40 percent cut of total branch office revenue "off the top" each month. Beck & Daniels managing attorneys in offices owned by the firm receive 20 percent of their local office's profit as their compensation. At other local offices managing attorneys (called local partners) buy a 92 percent stake in their office. Local partners must pay Beck & Daniels 8 percent of gross revenues each month and pay into regional advertising pools. In any case, managing attorneys are responsible for covering all office overhead, including the salaries of staff attorneys and secretaries, rental to the firms for furniture and equipment (including computers and their servicing), supplies (paper, pens, forms, etc.), office rental and utility costs and health and malpractice insurance.

Although both firms have similar compensation systems for managing attorneys, they package them quite differently. Arthur & Nelson managing attorneys are encouraged to view their position as negotiated with management and as relatively independent. They see themselves as earning profits for both themselves and the firm. Thus, Phil explains the compensation system as

work[ing] on the idea that a percentage of your profits goes to the law firm and a percentage stays with you. From that percentage you subtract your expenses and that's it. So for example, let's just say the office made $30,000 for the month, OK? So, if they took 35 percent of $30,000 what are we looking at, $10,500? That would leave you $19,000. If you subtracted your office expenses—let's say they ran $10,000—that would leave you a *profit* of $9,000 for the month. . . . So it's based on a percentage of what they take. *The percentages vary on the various managing attorneys that have come aboard in the various stages. So, they're all structured differently.* (emphasis added)

Beck & Daniels, on the other hand, encourages a view of managing attorneys as salaried employees. Managing attorneys are provided a minimum monthly income guarantee. In months when the office is not profitable enough to cover the guarantee, the managing attorney is provided with a steady income. In more profitable months the managing attorney is required to repay the "loan" forwarded by the firm. Beck & Daniels call the managing attorney's guarantee a "salary." The amount of the managing attorney's 20 percent of office profit that exceeds the guarantee is referred to as "bonus." In addition, bonuses are only paid on a quarterly basis. Thus managing attorneys at Beck & Daniels tend to view their guarantees as something they receive whether or not they earn it. Bonus is seen as a reward for high productivity rather than as part of the 20 percent of office profit they are entitled to in their contracts.[1]

Beck & Daniels attorneys are salaried; however, they do get a bonus. . . . You get your salary no matter how well or how poorly you do in any given month.

If you have a month where your revenues are low or your profits are low, depending on the situation, and you have a month where they are high—your profits are high, your revenues are high—the two months are going to be taken into consideration in determining whether or not you are entitled to a bonus. However, in no instance would they ask you to return any of your salary.

Both Arthur & Nelson's profit-based incentive system and Beck & Daniels' "salary" and "bonus" incentive system encourage managing attorneys to see their main role as creators of profits or revenue, not as attorneys serving client needs. Firm policies for evaluating local office performance reinforce this view. Like Carl, Arthur & Nelson managing attorneys find that branch offices are evaluated with

statistics on how many people you've seen, how many people you've retained, what kind of money you are earning, that kind of thing. . . . I never get any feedback other than statistics that they send me comparing this office . . . to other offices.

Client service is evaluated with periodic file audits and evaluation cards clients are asked to fill out and return by mail after they have bought a service. As Adam remarked, there is no real evaluation process "but there is an oversight process there."

My office as a whole gets reviewed on several different levels. My own work, not really. My office gets reviewed from an accounting point of view—they'll do an audit. From a trust point of view—they'll do a trust reconciliation audit. And, they will send down people to see if I'm using the right [administrative and accounting] forms. But my legal work qua legal work doesn't [get evaluated], not really. Sometimes I wish it was. I do have a superior, a district manager. . . . She does a file review. It's not so much to review my work, but to make sure no files are falling through the cracks. She does a file review probably two, three times a year. For the most part her suggestions are innocuous; send another letter, remind the clients they owe X amount of money.

When local offices earn high profits for the firm even the minimal file audits seem to disappear.

The district manager is supposed to do a yearly file audit. I saw [him] the other day and said, "so when are you coming by to audit my files?" He said, "in a couple of weeks probably." That was two months ago and he hasn't been by yet. File reviews don't always get done, especially if an office is doing well.

They keep their eye on the numbers.
That's all?
As far as I know. I had the supervisor's job for a while and I know what he has time to do. As long as the office is making money I'm the last guy he wants to look at. Although lately I haven't been making enough money, so maybe he is looking at me. I don't know.

The managing attorney's main role at franchise law firms is to operate a profitable office. Firm policies, incentive systems and evaluative systems all emphasize this main goal over the quality of client service. As we shall see, an important part of the managing attorney's job is to negotiate with management over the hiring and firing of support staff to create an environment where people work together as efficiently as possible.

Staff Attorneys

While the managing attorney's role is to ensure that the office is productive and profitable, staff attorneys are hired to consult with clients and sell services. In addition, staff attorneys often perform the legal tasks which are not directly revenue generating, such as going to court and conducting plaintiff's personal injury consultations (which generate fees only if a favorable settlement is reached through negotiations or the courts). Although staff attorneys may be delegated tasks by managing attorneys, most of their work is accomplished individually. Renee, a Beck & Daniels managing attorney, compares staff attorneys at her firm to associate attorneys at traditional law firms:

Unlike in a traditional law firm where you might have an owner or manager who basically takes in the cases and then farms the work out to his associates or to the nonpartners—he can call upon any of the nonpartners or associates to take his case or cover this or do that—here every Beck & Daniels attorney is responsible for his or her own cases. You don't have that option. You take a case on, it's your case and you handle it from start to finish.

Staff attorneys describe their responsibilities in a similar, though somewhat more harried, fashion. Rick and Jeff are staff attorneys at Arthur & Nelson and Beck & Daniels, respectively:

[I] just handle very large case loads. I don't know exactly how many but I'd say about 50, 60 files, and mainly divorce, bankruptcies—consumer bankruptcies—and other general, you know, wills, deeds, general practice, other things. Some litigation, civil litigation. Some criminal, but a majority of it's divorce and bankruptcies.

I do the intakes. When people come off the street and they want to see an attorney they see me or my boss. . . . Basically I get the less desirable cases to handle. So my job is to interview people and to figure out what their problem is and to make some kind of recommendation and to make a sale or just tell them that we can't help them.

Although staff attorneys have similar responsibilities at both Arthur & Nelson and Beck & Daniels, each firm has a distinct strategy for using staff attorneys. At Arthur & Nelson staff attorneys are extra help hired when managing attorneys believe they have more work than they (or secretaries) can handle. For managing attorneys the decision to hire a staff attorney is based on a cost-benefit equation. Will another attorney in the office increase revenue and profit? From the perspective of management, adding another attorney to an already successful office is a good way to increase gross revenues and the firm's take from that branch office. But for managing attorneys the decision is more complicated. Phil explains the dilemma as follows:

[Management] would love it for one reason: the more gross [revenues] you get, the more it helps the firm. But the more gross you do, if your expenses exceed what you're grossing, well, now your net is a little less than what you had and you have more work and more files. For example, if I take [an] attorney on who makes another $10,000 [in gross revenues], the firm gets its share off the top. But if my expenses are $10,000, what did I just do? I took on more work, more of a headache, and I'm not making the net. So you have to be careful.

Because the firm takes its cut of revenues off the top each month, managing attorneys remain responsible for the costs involved with staff attorney compensation and benefits. It is possible for Arthur & Nelson management to benefit from the hiring of staff attorneys while managing attorneys suffer.

While Arthur & Nelson managing attorneys find the hiring of staff attorneys to be a risky proposition, Beck & Daniels generally mandates at least one staff attorney to be present in each local office. To help ensure that an attorney is always available for client consultations, most Beck & Daniels offices have two or three staff attorneys. Traditionally, managing attorneys have had little control over the number of staff attorneys employed at their offices. Staffing policies have been mandated by upper management as part of the production system local offices must follow.[2]

Managing attorneys at both firms view staff attorney costs as overhead which may hurt branch office profits if not managed correctly. From the managing attorney's perspective it is necessary to have staff attorneys generate as much revenue as possible at a low cost to the office. This is accomplished in a number of ways. First, staff attorneys tend to be young, recent law school graduates who are entering an overcrowded labor market. For example, the average age of the staff attorneys I interviewed at Arthur & Nelson is 30; at Beck & Daniels the average age is 29.[3]

Second, staff attorneys begin to develop and service their own clients immediately upon being hired. Staff attorneys learn the practice of law through direct experience with virtually no formal training by the firm. As Rick put it,

you're given primary responsibility for case files the second you walk in the door. And that could mean taking a divorce from the initial stages and pleadings all the way through to a contested trial. Or it could mean writing up a couple of real estate contracts. It varies in the general practice area from that degree of basically office work to large strings of court appearances. And you do all that right away. It's not like a regular large firm where you'll be writing pleadings for your first few weeks, and then maybe they'll let you take some depositions, and then maybe some motion practice, and you won't go near a trial for at least two years into your experience with the firm.

Third, as is evident from virtually all of the quotations in this section, staff attorneys are constantly working: seeing clients, drafting court motions and other documents for their managing attorneys, and going to court. Arthur & Nelson staff attorneys report working an average of 57 hours each week. Beck & Daniels requires staff attorneys to work a minimum of 45 hours each week. Yet firm requirements that branch office attorneys remain available to clients during specific hours each day means that staff attorneys such as Jeff often put in another ten hours each week.

I put in anywhere from 50 to 60 [hours] each week. I think I put in more than I'm required to. . . . If I have something to do I'm going to come in and do it. I never take lunch either, which is kind of a bad habit. I kind of eat while I'm doing work and its not real healthy. I need to start taking some time off—just getting out of the office for half an hour or whatever.

Finally, while being kept busy for relatively long hours, staff attorney salaries are kept low. For example, my sample of Arthur & Nelson staff attorneys have an average annual income of $29,000. At Beck & Daniels the salaries are kept even lower, averaging $21,250. Beck & Daniels staff attorneys are told that while the salary is low, they may earn bonuses based on the revenue they generate each month. During the period of the study, staff attorneys earned 27 percent of all revenues in excess of $8,700 they brought into the firm each month. However, combining bonus and salary, staff attorneys still only report average annual incomes of $23,000. Staff attorneys at both firms feel as though they are thrown into a lion's den without proper compensation for their efforts. Mike, a staff attorney employed by Beck & Daniels, focuses upon the low salary in his assessment of the firm:

The salary is terrible. It's very aggravating. I mean, I'm just way overworked, and the hours I work—that's my main complaint about the job in addition to the salary—there are just too many cases to really do a good job.

At Arthur & Nelson (where salaries are slighly higher), Josh is more concerned about the long hours he works:

It's one thing to say that you can expect to periodically put in some time, but just consistently long hours! I think once, a while back, I was just trying to add up all the hours that I put in—not in a week, but in a month's period of time—and then say, the return here, is it really worth it?

This intense exploitation of staff attorneys would not be possible without an overcrowded labor market. Phil, who is particularly clear on this topic, explains the role of the legal labor market in his successful practice with Arthur & Nelson:

There's a great resource out there of young attorneys. Every year the law schools are turning them out. Huge amounts, right? This year we're going to have maybe 4,000–5,000 passing the bar, being admitted and looking for jobs. They're willing—we started [my staff attorney] at the salary of $24,000. They're willing to work for $24,000 for the experience alone! Law school has been 50 percent of what they're doing. Now it's actual practice. It's dealing with people. It's all the guidelines that they can't do alone. We're almost at a point where, if we wanted to, we could be like the medical profession and drive them down to an intern's fee of $15,000 or $10,000 because of the need for experience. And it's getting to be that way because there is a huge surplus of young attorneys out there. I don't actually need an expert attorney. In one year he becomes pretty good. I need him to do all the work that's necessary for fill-ins. If it's a serious case, I'll handle it. I could turn over an attorney every two years, and that's the way it works.

Perhaps the most telling comparison is the relative worth of secretaries versus staff attorneys at franchise law firms. Secretarial salaries range from $16,000 to $36,000 while staff attorney compensation ranges include a low of $14,000 to a high of $36,000. Staff attorney compensation is comparable to, and in some cases lower than, secretarial compensation. Indeed, most managing attorneys admit that secretaries are more important to branch office productivity and profits than are staff attorneys.

Secretaries

Secretaries are instrumental to operating successful branch offices. Secretaries wear many hats, providing services wherever they are needed. The different tasks performed by secretaries include dealing with incoming cash and accounting procedures, ordering office supplies, updating clients on the current disposition of their cases, motivating potential clients who telephone to make appointments, screening out undesirable potential clients, creating and copying documents, writing letters to clients and producing wills and other legal forms. As one managing attorney put it, a secretary is

a jack of all trades. Obviously, the initial client contact is through her; she sets up appointments. She has them [clients] fill out the initial consultation sheet that we have them do. She handles all the money coming into the firm in terms of payment of retainers and ongoing payments on cases. And she handles a lot of the administrative red tape, for example, submitting petty cash requests, keeping track of the trust fund information and the general disbursements fund, the business account, things of that nature.

In addition to the tasks mentioned above, secretaries at Beck & Daniels branch offices also control an elaborate computer system that is used for producing legal documents and letters, tracking clients, and keeping contact with the home office. The two roles of operating the computer system and dealing with clients are considered distinct enough that most Beck & Daniels branch offices have two full-time secretaries who switch between answering the telephone and dealing with clients in the office and producing legal forms and documents on the computer system. Managing attorneys learn to view secretaries as essential partners in operating branch offices. For example, Carl at Arthur & Nelson has found that

a secretary plays a big role if you've got a good one. She can make your job a lot easier and a lot more enjoyable. . . . She can play a role to screen clients and taking questions as opposed to just putting questions through [to the attorney]. I think that's important. It's very easy to say, "Well, he's not here can I take a message?" and come back with a big stack of messages. Whereas my secretary will say, "He's not here, is there something I can help you with?" to try to alleviate a lot of the messages. The secretary plays a big role.

It is important to point out that while secretaries perform many "paralegal" duties, neither Beck & Daniels nor Arthur & Nelson employ certified paralegals. Management at each firm regards paralegals to be too expensive and too narrowly trained to serve the needs of local offices. Franchise law firms create "legal assistants" suited to the requirements of franchise practice through on-the-job training of novice secretaries.

Despite their lack of legal training, it does not take long for secretaries to realize their importance to branch office success. Secretaries describe their responsibilities as "doing everything" necessary to keep the branch office operating. Many refer to their role as being the unofficial "office manager." Sarah (Beck & Daniels) and Sandy (Arthur & Nelson) provide typical examples of secretary experiences at franchise law firms:

Oh my, I do everything. I type, I file, book appointments. I handle all the cash flow. I greet clients. I meet clients. I do financial affidavits for divorce clients. I do everything. I copy, I file, I order supplies, I maintain supplies. . . . I do everything except for go[ing] to court.

I run the office, let's put it that way. My boss would be lost without me. I do almost everything in the office except interview the clients. All the paperwork is done by me. Everything is done by me and I run the office. I order supplies, I take care of petty cash. I take care of a lot of things that the managing attorney does not take care of.

The compensation systems reflect the critical role of secretaries in office production. Secretaries are salaried rather than hourly employees. This serves to insulate the secretaries somewhat from the peaks and valleys of income that managing attorneys may experience. To help motivate secretaries, both firms require managing attorneys to pay bonuses based on each office's monthly revenues. Yet the compensation system also serves another purpose. It allows managing attorneys to work secretaries for long hours without increasing their pay. This helps managing attorneys to minimize labor costs while exploiting secretaries to the fullest possible extent. Phil at Arthur & Nelson relates how secretaries are best utilized as he explains why he is not burdened by administrative work:

We have very good assistants who eliminate a lot of that [administrative] work. The secretary is able to give [the administrative office] the information they need about what clients are coming in, who is retained. And that sheet she fills out with the retainer [paid by the client] and the [balance due] statement practically shows everything. . . . The point that the managing attorney has is, number one, to be here, to constantly see people, to work his files and his clients, *and to make sure the secretaries are constantly busy. . . . The idea is we have that constant flow of work.* (emphasis added)

For their average annual incomes of $26,000 and $18,000 at Arthur & Nelson and Beck & Daniels, respectively, secretaries are required to work 37.5 hours each week. However, branch office secretaries generally give beyond the call of duty. Secretaries at Arthur & Nelson (the only firm I have this data for) report working a minimum of 40 hours and an average of 50 hours each week. Given the volume of work and diversity of tasks completed by secretaries as part of their regular duties, it is no wonder that managing attorneys prefer to lose staff attorneys rather than experienced secretaries from their offices.

THE EVOLVING MASS PRODUCTION MODEL

In this chapter I have described the basic organizational model franchise law firms have developed. It is clear that secretaries aided by computer boilerplate are the essential element in office productivity. Staff attorneys are neither essential nor considered to be legal experts. They are extra help to facilitate selling services to clients. Managing attorneys also engage in the sales process through consultations with clients (see Chapter 3). But the main role of managing attorneys is to supervise secretaries and staff attorneys, and take the economic risks inherent in operating branch offices.

Managing attorneys and firm management rely upon one another to help assure the smooth operation of the law firm and the earning of profits. For example, Arthur & Nelson and Beck & Daniels managements develop nationally or regionally disseminated advertising campaigns. Managing attorneys have virtually no input with advertising strategy. Managing attorneys expect that firm owners and managers will develop campaigns which will bring clients to their local offices to buy services provided at those offices. In return, management expects local offices to adhere to firm policies and production standards when dealing with clients. However, during the course of this study both Beck & Daniels and Arthur & Nelson sought to rationalize client services beyond the basic franchise models described earlier in the chapter. The changes instituted at each law firm are quite different—Beck & Daniels franchised its offices; Arthur & Nelson developed special units which circumvent branch offices. Despite these differences, both firms were reacting to disgruntled local office employees and the 1990s economic downturn in the legal services industry.

By the 1990s the legal services industry began to stagnate. Large law firms that had prospered in the 1980s began to fail (Brill 1989; Nelson and Trubek 1992). The legal press carried stories reporting layoffs at law firms (Brill 1991a; Clarke 1991) and announcing the end of the legal services boom of the 1980s (Brill 1991b; Rutman 1991). Arthur & Nelson was stagnating. By 1993 the firm was closing as many branch offices as it opened. Beck & Daniels was in decline and had closed more than half of its local offices by 1993.

Arthur & Nelson

The basic franchise model involves local offices which offer services to clients based on production systems and criteria determined by law firm management. As long as the law firm successfully and responsibly advertises for services available at the local offices, both management and branch offices potentially benefit. Prior to reorganizing, Arthur & Nelson focused its advertising and branch office production on the area of family law, particularly divorce. During the recession, however, family law ceased to be as lucrative as it had been. Arthur & Nelson management chose to change the direction of emphasis of the law firm to other areas of personal legal services. Specifically, it decided to develop personal bankruptcy and personal injury emphases. But rather than "retool" and retrain branch office attorneys and secretaries for these new areas of legal practice, Arthur & Nelson developed a system of special units to process case files which initiated at branch offices.[4]

Similar to branch offices in organization, special units rely upon support staff to perform many of the routine tasks. Generally, a few attorneys supervise a large cohort of secretaries. Kent, a former personal injury unit staff attorney explains that

the unit actually gets run by mirrors. There are a heck of a lot of support staff and not a lot of attorneys. There is one managing attorney. When I left I was one of two attorneys who actually handled files. The bulk of the files were in the hands of the paralegals. . . . Each attorney had a handful of paralegals and each paralegal held close to 100 files. So while I had my own case load that I would handle in a normal fashion—just trying to negotiate, try and settle, or . . . do the litigation, arbitration or whatever—there were a lot of responsibilities for supervising the paralegals and the files they had. They would handle the files for the first six months to a year. I had to make sure that they were doing that properly because they were only trained on the job as paralegals. They certainly did not have a law degree! Most of them did not even have paralegal degrees, for what good that does.

From the time a file would come in—it would come into the branch office, it would get transferred to us, the file would be open—it would be assigned to an attorney and paralegal. At that point the attorney would review the file [and] tell the paralegal what had to be done up front. The paralegal would have to make sure the client was going to the doctor, resolve the property damage, order the investigation, [and] set up the claims with the insurance company on both sides. Basically, the paralegal would run the file until the person was either done treating or it was, for statute reasons or whatever, to be put into [a law] suit.

To increase productivity further, Arthur & Nelson invested in computer systems and developed software for the specific needs of the bankruptcy and personal injury units. For example, the firm has "internally developed" "a series of bankruptcy programs where there's a tracking system to keep track of all the bankruptcy clients." In addition to these programs, the "staff has three or four word processors" with specific programs that are used to produce standardized forms and letters.

By focusing more of its resources on the personal bankruptcy and personal injury units, Arthur & Nelson expanded its clientele and centralized its case file processing. Centralizing production offers a number of benefits. First, by centralizing negotiations with creditors (for bankruptcy) and insurance companies (for personal injury) the firm is able to develop ongoing contacts and become a "repeat player" (Galanter 1974) in those arenas. Repeat players have more success in legal arenas because their continuing contact allows them to develop specific knowledge and personal ties related to obtaining the desired outcome. "One-shotters" or less frequent players may not be able to develop the same level of knowledge or resources simply because they are not involved in the process on a regular basis (Galanter 1974). Branch office attorneys tend to become repeat players for divorce negotiations (though not at centralized locations). Special units allow the firm to develop similar relationships for personal injury (PI) and bankruptcy cases.

Second, centralized production offers management greater control over the work process. For example, attorneys working in personal injury units complain that Arthur & Nelson management limits the number of cases they may litigate and sets quotas for settling cases. Bill, another former personal injury unit staff attorney, explains the limits imposed on his practice:

The system only works if the attorneys are in the office at almost all times. So our job was to make sure that we stayed in the office. To do that you couldn't litigate a lot of cases. So there were, for a large part of the time I was there, there were imposed caps in the number of cases that could be put into suit for any one attorney at any one time. They'd push the paralegals to get people to finish treating and wrap up getting their medicals. Then they would push us to try and settle cases. They'd push the accounting people to get the money in the door. . . . As far as trying to settle cases, settlement was stressed a lot more there than it is in most PI [personal injury] firms. It was my major function as far as they were concerned. Their viewpoint was, "Well for those few cases that you can't settle, you'll have to put them into suit and do [litigate] those.

As the above quote suggests, special units emphasize processing routine (e.g., non-litigated) cases as quickly and efficiently as possible. By using support staff and computers to process the large number of cases channeled to them from branch offices, special units take advantage of increased productivity and better control over the work force.

The third benefit of centralizing production in special units is lower overhead costs. By processing bankruptcy and PI cases at centralized locations, management need not supply all branch offices with the necessary staff, computers and software. Branch office attorneys and secretaries complain that the firm is "stuck in the dark ages" of technology, while special units are "made nicer, better offices."

Finally, centralized production makes it possible to develop new clients, more efficient production techniques and lower overhead costs in a manner that benefits firm management more than branch offices. Arthur & Nelson's network of branch offices provides clients with convenient access to all available services. But by removing the processing of lucrative cases to special units, management deprives branch offices of most of the revenues and profits generated by those cases. Although branch offices are required to perform initial consultations for clients whose case files are sent to special units, their only compensation is a small referral fee which is determined by management.

Beck & Daniels

Beck & Daniels' reorganization, called the local partner initiative, follows from the premise that better, more dedicated branch office managing attorneys are necessary to make the existing production system function in a profitable manner. As the managing partner of the law firm explains it, the local partner initiative,

involves the installation of equity partners at our [branch] offices. Historically, the local office managing attorney has been an employee of the firm with some profit participation, but not ownership. Our local partners will be owners of their offices and the profits from their operations will belong to them.

With local partnership, successful managing attorneys, regional managers and national managers are offered the opportunity to buy a "controlling" interest (92 percent) in one or more branch offices. Unprofitable offices and offices for which there are no buyers are closed. In buying their offices managing attorneys gain more responsibility for office operations. Local partners take over staff hiring and salary decisions. In addition, payroll and other disbursements are also handled locally. For most managing attorneys who become local partners the change in status from employee to owner is very important. Eric is a typical example.

I guess, very simply, . . . you become an owner-operator, for want of a better term, of an office and you pretty much take over an office lock, stock and barrel. The employees work for you. You pay them. You give them benefits. You maintain independent malpractice insurance. You run the office as if it was yours. There is contact with Beck & Daniels . . . but for all practical purposes, from a business standpoint, it really is my office.

It is interesting to note that, with the exception of hiring and firing decisions, managing attorneys have always been responsible for fulfilling the duties mentioned in the above quote. As discussed earlier in this chapter, all managing attorneys have to generate sufficient revenues to pay employees and other overhead costs—including insurance. Local partners simply accept responsibility for paying the bills directly from their offices. In addition, Beck & Daniels retains an 8 percent stake in each office as well as control over television advertising, production systems, technology and revenue goals. Local partners must service the debt from their equity buy-in (which is often financed by the firm); they must pay 8 percent of monthly gross revenues and an additional monthly advertising fee to the firm. Failure to fulfill any number of responsibilities may result in the loss of partnership. Matt explains:

What happened is . . . they asked me if I wanted to become a partner, and really, you know, it was very expensive to buy a partnership. I mean, I paid a hundred and something thousand dollars for this office. . . . And basically, I pay quite a lot of money for the advertising, plus I pay 8 percent of my revenues to them. Every Tuesday they electronically transfer from my bank account—because I gave them limited power of attorney to do so—8 percent of my revenues plus an advertising fee. The advertising fee is fixed based on the number of offices [in an advertising district]. Like we have nine offices in this area. But the 8 percent is not fixed. You have a minimum, a minimum [revenue] requirement that you have to meet, and I think that's $16,000 a month. Eight percent of $16,000 a month or they can pull your partnership agreement away.

In addition to the economic issues, partnership agreements ensure that the nature or character of branch offices, including production and computer systems, services provided and the hours each office remains open, remains unchanged. Beck & Daniels' managing partner emphasizes that

how we provide affordable and convenient access to the legal system to middle-income people will not change. The local partner does not take down the sign, destroy the letterhead, and become a personal injury firm or a litigation firm or a firm that specializes in employment discrimination and complex litigation. He operates a Beck & Daniels office consistent with the standards set forth in the partnership agreement, all of which require him to maintain the essential character of the office. So . . . I think our local partners believe that they have more autonomy, more freedom, greater control of their office operations, but understand pretty clearly that the nature of the practice has not changed.

Local partners confirm that the operations manual has not been discarded:

Oh yeah, yeah, it's still the same standard system for all the Beck & Daniels offices, and, you know, we also have to remain open 9:00 to 8:00 Monday through Thursday, 9:00 to 6:00 on Fridays, and 9:00 to 4:00 on Saturdays.

As far as hours of operation, case types that we have to offer, representation, yeah, there is an office procedures manual as far as file management, accounting, what not, sure.

To help assure that the Beck & Daniels production system will remain in use, management requires each local office to purchase a new computer system that links the corporate headquarters to each office. The computer system provides branch offices with the forms and programs previously developed by the firm and allows management to check up on branch offices on a daily basis. Management can use the computer network to check branch office revenues as well as case types that the office has recently performed work on. Management also uses the computer system to calculate and collect its royalties and advertising fees each week. Many local partners view the computer system as a symbol of their lack of control over their legal work—past and present. Frank's complaint's are typical among local partners and managing attorneys:

We had no input on the computer system that we got. Right now, in the different regions, there are three computer systems being used. The original, the one that I was brought in with, is a ten-year-old or a twelve-year-old Wang system which makes a God-awful noise when it goes off and is very slow. And it's very expensive to keep up. Then there's the LINDA [computer system] which I happen to love. I thought I'd go through life being computer illiterate and I fought tooth and nail when they insisted that I be trained on the LINDA system. But I got trained on it and I became good at it and I really enjoyed it. I thought it was just fine.

Now the local partnership offices, for the most part, have been put onto what they call the LOIS system. That's where we are now. [Management] knows quite well I hate it. I truly hate it. . . . We had no say at all, none whatsoever. This is what we are getting. If we are going to get the offices we're obligated to purchase [the LOIS system]. As a managing attorney I could have accepted that. . . . [But now] it is important for them to ask us. And it is important to us that they hear what we have to say, because, still, *with partnership we don't have the unrestricted authority to go ahead and just do things the way we want to if we don't think that what [management] is suggesting is the best way to do it.* (emphasis added)

Despite buying a controlling interest in branch offices, partnership agreements allow Beck & Daniels to maintain tight control over the operation of branch offices. Beck & Daniels local partner initiative assumes, as the firm's managing partner put it, that "we've always had great systems to represent . . . clients efficiently, competently and profitably." Because management retains control over advertising, production techniques and technology and revenue standards, many local partners refer to Beck & Daniels as a franchise. For example, Lorna argues that her position is "set up basically like a franchise . . . but they claim it's a partnership." Such a view is not unwarranted. Local partners contract to use the Beck & Daniels name, production and technology systems to provide legal services to consumers targeted by the firm. In return, local partners agree to pay management a royalty of 8 percent of gross revenues and to operate local offices to Beck & Daniels' specifications. Even Beck & Daniels' managing partner admits that the "economic parallels between . . . a franchise and our new partnership structure are pretty obvious."

For the founding partners of the law firm the local partnership initiative has been a way to raise capital quickly and begin expanding the law firm again while local partners burden the risk. As a national manager explains, local partnership is

a really great method of raising capital. It also is an opportunity to expand the law firm using other people's capital to do so. In the history of our firm [the founding partners] have been brilliant in being able at every point where there has been an expansion of the firm to do it basically without any of their own money. And this is another opportunity to do that.

But to the local partners it appears that there is no longer a "law firm." Instead the founding partners are now profiting by selling production and technology systems for processing specific legal case types. In Matt's estimation management has used the reorganization of the law firm as "an opportunity to alleviate a lot of the headaches . . . from a centralized management type of organization" as well as "an opportunity to drastically reduce their overhead. Those people are pretty damn smart . . . for better or for worse."

Beck & Daniels and Arthur & Nelson have developed networks of branch offices based on concepts of rational organization to deliver legal services to consumers. The organization of work and incentives at these firms assigns specific responsibilities and duties to each of the three positions found in branch offices. Managing attorneys are responsible for the day-to-day operation of local offices. They are clearly focused on productivity and profits. Staff attorneys are not essential staff. Rather, they are extra help for managing attorneys to ensure that clients meet with an attorney without a long wait for an appointment. Staff attorneys are not required or expected to be legal experts. They tend to be young, new law school graduates who have encountered a difficult job market. Secretaries at franchise law firms have the broadest range of tasks and responsibilities. They are acknowledged by all attorneys to be essential to the operation of branch offices. Although managing attorneys assume the economic risks of operating branch offices, secretaries make them run smoothly, efficiently and profitably. One of the most telling indicators of the relative importance of secretaries versus staff attorneys is their levels of compensation. Secretarial compensation is comparable to, and in some cases exceeds, staff attorney compensation levels.

Local offices are organized around task-oriented production systems and are capable of processing a large number of clients on a regular basis. Nonetheless, Arthur & Nelson and Beck & Daniels have sought to further increase productivity and lower costs. Arthur & Nelson has created special units to process personal bankruptcy and personal injury claims. Special units centralize production, offering greater managerial control, higher rates of productivity and lower overhead costs. Special units pose a dilemma for branch offices because they have the potential to remove all skilled work from branch offices and reduce attorneys to nothing more than intake workers (see Chapter 5).

Beck & Daniels has followed a different path, selling local offices to managing attorneys. The local partner initiative does not significantly alter the work performed at branch offices. In fact, Beck & Daniels management has gone to lengths to make sure that the character of branch office work remains unchanged. Rather than giving branch offices more autonomy, local partnership asks managing attorneys to pay for the privilege of continuing to use Beck & Daniels' name and highly specified production systems. Nonetheless, local partnership appears to elicit greater satisfaction from managing attorneys who are taking greater economic risks while accomplishing the same tasks as managing attorneys who have no equity investment (see chapters 5 and 6).

In the next chapter I examine the process of serving clients who come to Arthur & Nelson and Beck & Daniels branch offices for legal services. Despite some organizational and technology differences between the two firms, similar practices are applied to client services.

NOTES

1. Arthur & Nelson also provides its managing attorneys with a guaranteed income to cover unprofitable months. However, Arthur & Nelson managing attorneys are encouraged by firm management to view the guarantee as a loan, not a salary.

2. Staffing policies are discussed in more detail in Chapters 5 and 6.

3. These ages exclude one 50-year-old and one 44-year-old staff attorney at Arthur & Nelson and Beck & Daniels, respectively. Despite his age, the 50-year-old staff attorney was a recent law school graduate. The 44-year-old was more experienced but was in training for a Beck & Daniels managing attorney position.

4. Arthur & Nelson currently has three special units: personal bankruptcy, personal injury and criminal. Most of my discussion in this book is limited to the personal bankruptcy and personal injury units.

3

Client Services: Selling and Processing Law

One of the most important aspects of any professional practice is the delivery of services to clients. Franchise law firm advertisements claim to offer clients uniquely personal services. Potential clients are told that "the law" and legal systems can be cold and confusing. Franchise law firms offer to hold the client's hand and walk him through our "maze of laws."

This chapter[1] explores how franchise law firms fulfill such promises. From the advertising pitches to the delivery of the final product, clients are led down a well-planned and tightly controlled path. Ironically, it is salemanship—not legal skills—that lawyers and secretaries develop that allow a limited and routinized set of services to be experienced as personalized service and hand-holding by clients. I begin with a brief examination of the functions of television advertising for franchise law firms. I then discuss how clients, secretaries and lawyers interact in branch offices through the sale and production of services. The chapter concludes with a discussion of how clients experience their interactions with franchise law firms.

ADVERTISING AND ONE-SHOT CLIENTS

In contrast to most of their competitors, franchise law firms rely heavily upon television advertising to tap new clients. Indeed, both Arthur & Nelson and Beck & Daniels pioneered television advertising by lawyers after the U.S. Supreme Court struck down bar association prohibitions on advertising in 1977.

The content of the advertising message, the time of day (or night) advertisements air and even which television stations they appear on helps to determine the characteristics of the clientele that will contact branch offices. The sometimes controversial advertisements of franchise law firms are carefully crafted to encourage individuals who have never before sought out legal services to do so now. The messages offer friendly advice and services for a low cost. The advertisements are intended to appeal to consumers who might choose a lawyer based on the *price* of the consultation rather than through family, friend or work-related networks.

Television advertising results in three major benefits for franchise law firms. First, it supplies a steady flow of clients to branch offices. This is important because the competitive fees charged by franchise law firms often have very small profit margins. Franchise law firms rely on developing economies of scale for their most basic services. In addition, personal services lawyers often cannot rely on repeat business. This is particularly true of franchise law firms which encourage "one-shotters" (Galanter 1974)—clients who may seek out legal services only once during their lifetimes. As Frank, a Beck & Daniels local partner, explains, the nature of the work offers few opportunities to garner repeat business:

Because of the nature of our service, it's not the kind of a case where the client would keep you on retainer, because a person who needs a will is not going to need a will every year.

Beck & Daniels and Arthur & Nelson attorneys estimate that, at best, ten to fifteen previous clients will return for new services in any year.

A second benefit of television advertising for franchise law firms is that it insulates branch offices from the rather intense competition for clients among personal services lawyers in metropolitan areas. For example, Arthur & Nelson attorneys report that they perceive little competition with local lawyers:

You see, everyone—every single practitioner, every lawyer—is out there scrambling for business. I don't have to go out and scramble for clients. Arthur & Nelson advertises and that's how you get your clients. So no, I'm not aware of [competition], although I know generally there's a very sharp competition for clients.

I guess the law's become a competitive business, but I don't really sense anything. . . . No one competes in advertising along the same lines that we do, and that's why I say I don't feel any competition.

Arthur & Nelson managing attorneys often point to the connection between television advertising and the number of clients who seek out services. Phil offers a typical discussion:

We rely very heavily on our television advertising to bring people in. And . . . we can see very often, [and] there are times when people from the regional office will admit, that [when] advertising goes up, client flow goes up. And they can almost see within a period of a month to six weeks a direct correlation.

Beck & Daniels attorneys are even more enthusiatic about the positive effects of advertising.

I would say that there is . . . some hostility about Beck & Daniels taking the share of the market that they do among other lawyers. . . . I find when I reach a new lawyer that there is an initial bristling hostility which usually can be overcome. . . . I know we take clients who would go to them otherwise. Obviously, television advertising works!

I think that a lot of the lawyers have bad-mouthed Beck & Daniels as like the K-Mart of the legal profession, or, you know, that it's a retail type of practice. But I think the reason why they did that is because we were basically closing down the sole practitioners, because we had the national backing to advertise, which is very expensive.

I can find no support for the claim that franchise law firms "close down the sole practitioners." Nonetheless, it seems clear that the level of advertising engaged in by these firms insulates branch offices from much of the competition that characterizes other types of personal legal services practices.

Finally, the one-shotters pursued by franchise law firms through television advertising have little, if any, experience with lawyers. Clients are often engaged in blue-collar or white-collar occupations, earn lower-middle incomes and have no more than high school level educations. As we shall see, these clients do not expect to work with an attorney to solve their problems. Instead, they expect the attorney to have solutions to their problems. Such expectations fit nicely with the franchise law firm's limited menu of services, sales orientation and efficient production procedures.

In many ways franchise law firms are organized around taking advantage of television advertising. However, it is important to point out that television advertising also creates challenges which branch offices must overcome. One of these challenges has to do with undesirable clients. Desirable clients have a specific legal problem that a branch office is equipped to deal with and are financially capable of paying for any services they purchase. Television advertising reaches a wide variety of individuals who may not be viewed as appropriate clients. Secretaries and attorneys spend a significant amount of time screening out those who are seeking to sue the president for covering up the existence of UFOs, alcoholics and others who do not have a specific legal problem but simply want someone to talk to, and those who cannot afford to purchase legal services. Secretaries often find they must strike a balance between encouraging individuals who appear to be appropriate potential clients to make appointments, and ascertaining enough information to turn away undesirable clients.

BRINGING THE CLIENTS IN

At the branch office it is the secretary who usually makes first contact with clients. In Chapter 2 we saw that managing attorneys place much emphasis on the ability of secretaries to book clients into their offices, and that secretaries take this responsibility quite seriously. Secretaries try to take whatever action is necessary to convince callers to schedule appointments. This may include offering estimates of the average costs of services, suggesting possible payment plans and even dispensing basic legal advice (whether correct or not). For example, during my office visits with Arthur & Nelson, Jennifer responded to a caller shopping for a divorce as follows:

I'm sorry sir, I cannot tell you exactly how much a divorce will cost you. You will have to see the attorney and she will provide you with a written fee estimate after she determines what you need. Our initial consultation fee is $35. (Pause) Yes, it will cost you $35 to talk to the attorney and have her tell you how much it will cost to retain our services. If you retain us for the divorce within 24 hours after talking to the attorney, the initial fee, the $35 will be credited toward your retainer. (Pause) Right, yes, if you come back to us within 24 hours the initial fee will be credited toward your retainer. Would you like to schedule an appointment with the attorney? (Pause) No, I can't estimate . . . (Pause) Well, all I can tell you is that our average fee for a divorce is $1500. Your case may be a little more, but in my experience most people don't have to pay more than that. (Pause) You would? When would you like to come in?

On another occasion a secretary explained to a potential client that if they retained an attorney's services, but could not afford to pay the retainer up front, the office would allow them to put one-third down and pay the remainder in monthly installments. When I asked the secretary if such a plan was office policy, she admitted that only the managing attorney may make payment plan determinations. In fact, managing attorneys often require that new clients pay at least half the retainer up front before any work may begin. A client must make a very good impression before many managing attorneys will agree to payment plans. Nevertheless, the secretary maintained that she was only explaining potential options in the best possible light, and an appointment was scheduled.

As secretaries gain experience dealing with legal issues and learn basic legal concepts they may also dispense basic legal advice to help put worried people at ease and motivate them to make appointments. In the following example from my field notes, the secretary is especially motivated because the firm pays her a bonus for every potential personal injury client she books into the office:

bonuses
For
sec'y

The telephone rings. Ginny answers, "Arthur & Nelson, how may I help you?" After a moment of listening into the phone Ginny's eyes widen and she says "Ma'am, do you have collision insurance? Is your son covered for collision? Is your daughter covered for collision? Yes? Then you have nothing to worry about, you're covered. You're covered. What's the problem? The initial consultation is $35, but what are you going to talk to the lawyer about? You're covered! What's the problem?" Ginny holds the phone away from her ear for a few moments. "Ma'am listen to me." Ginny listens for a moment, then holds the phone away again. "Is the nose broken? Is the nose broken? Ma'am listen to me. *Are there any broken bones? If there are broken bones you have a personal injury case. If there are no broken bones you're covered by insurance and you shouldn't worry about it.* That's right, if there are broken bones. But if there are broken bones you have a case, so why don't you make an appointment with the lawyer? It doesn't cost you anything to see a lawyer for personal injury cases. Ma'am, listen to me. If the nose is broken you have a personal injury case. Is the nose broken? Is the nose broken? You don't know yet? Well, if it's broken you have a case and should come in to talk with a lawyer. Yes. OK, you can call back." (emphasis added)

Beck & Daniels' secretaries are somewhat more restrained in their telephone conversations with clients than are secretaries at Arthur & Nelson. Firm rules generally prohibit secretaries from providing fee quotes or dispensing legal advice. Secretaries emphasize to clients that they may speak to a qualified attorney about any legal problem for only $20. Although it is not necessarily true that clients will be allowed to speak with an attorney "about any legal problem," I rarely witnessed secretaries offering legal advice over the telephone. At most, secretaries tell clients what types of services are available at branch offices. However, because clients often do not know if they have a problem that may be solved through legal means, secretaries encourage most callers to simply schedule an appointment. If a potential client is persistent about wanting more information, secretaries may ask an attorney who is not busy to field their questions and help persuade them to schedule an appointment. In addition to the low initial consultation fee, secretaries motivate clients by explaining that the consultation fee may be applied to the cost of any services purchased within 48 hours of the consultation, and that payment plans are also available (as in the quote from Jennifer above). Nonetheless, during my office visits, a Beck & Daniels secretary complained that "it would be a lot easier to get people to come in here if we could tell them how much their case might cost and reassure them more."

AT THE OFFICE

When clients first enter a branch office, they are greeted by a secretary and asked to fill out an initial consultation form. The form asks clients to report identifying information, including their name, address, phone number, information about their employer, and to briefly describe their problem. It is the responsibility of secretaries to determine what type of legal problem (or problems) clients have. Once a case type is determined, it is written in code on the initial consultation form.

When attorneys are assigned new clients they use the initial consultation forms to prepare for the meeting. The attorney may check the fee schedule or gather relevant forms or worksheets based on the case types determined earlier by the secretary.

During the consultation the attorney must verify the client's legal problem and ascertain relevant information from the client in a timely manner. Both firms supply their attorneys with worksheets containing questions to ask clients for most types of cases to streamline the process and help make sure that all necessary information is gathered at the first meeting. During the consultations I observed, attorneys appeared to use these worksheets to keep clients from what one attorney called, "telling their whole life stories." This is especially important for attorneys when the clients are emotionally upset—for example, those who are seeking a divorce—since entire consultations average no more than fifteen or twenty minutes.

After watching Phil, an Arthur & Nelson managing attorney, complete consultations with four clients in the course of one hour (and successfully sell services to all of them), I asked him if he was able to spend enough time with the clients. He replied, "listen, I'm not interested in their life stories. When you have people scheduled only 15 minutes apart, I don't have time for it and it's not necessary." Another Arthur & Nelson attorney explains that "at 150 dollars an hour our consultation fee [of $35] doesn't even buy 15 minutes—and I sometimes give them 20 minutes." Similarly, a Beck & Daniels managing attorney argues that "the initial consultation fee [of $20] buys about 11 minutes, but you can't do an IC in less than 15."

The following extended example of a typical divorce consultation shows how worksheets are used to help control the interaction and keep consultations short. Sara, a woman in her early thirties, is guided into a small office by Sam, a Beck & Daniels managing attorney, who quietly closes the door behind him. Sara sits and stares at the floor. Sam takes his seat behind his desk, looks at the initial consultation form for a moment and then says, "You want a divorce, is that right?" Sara responds, "Well, I'm pretty unhappy. Jim, my husband, is out of work. He's drinking again and we fight all the time. . . ." "Are you still living with him?" Sam interrupts. Sara says she is because she only recently began to seriously consider divorce as an option. Sam interrupts again, "Why don't you let me get some basic information that we're going to need to file a motion for divorce and then I can tell you how it will work and estimate the cost. OK?" Sam goes down the worksheet asking questions, circling and writing answers as Sara responds. "Do you have any children? Two? What are their full names? How old are they? Is your husband unemployed or laid off? Is he drawing unemployment? How much per month? I see you work also. What is your job? What are your monthly earnings? Do you own a home or rent? Do you have any cars? How much is currently in your joint checking account? Savings? Do you have any other assests?"

Sara quietly answers all of the questions. Her children are three and six years of age. Her husband receives about $500 each month from unemployment. She works part-time as a secretary and earns about $500 a month. They don't own a home. There is not much left in the checking or savings accounts with Jim having been out of work for almost a year.

Once he has completed the worksheet, Sam begins a well-rehearsed monologue:

OK, let me explain how it works. In this state we have uncontested or no-fault divorce. Any spouse can file and be granted a motion for dissolution of the marriage without the other's consent. But we don't have community property in this state. That means you and your husband have to be able to agree to a property settlement. Do you think the two of you can agree on that? It shouldn't be too difficult since you don't own a home or any assests. If you think he might come into the office and sign a form agreeing to a 50–50 split of your household that would be the easiest way to go. [Sara says she doesn't know if Jim will sign such an agreement.] Well, that would be the easiest and least expensive. Try, and if he signs, great. If not, we can still do it, it will just cost a little more.

Now with the children the courts usually award joint custody. Usually the mother is given physical custody and that is what we will ask for since you said he has an alcohol problem. Now I want you to understand that the courts use a formula to set child support responsibilities. The formula is based on each parent's income. I want you to understand that the court will find that you are responsible for half of their support, OK?

OK, now for the cost. If he agrees to a property settlement and joint custody, with you having physical custody of the children, and I only have to make two appearances in court I can do the divorce for $1200. That includes filling out all the court forms and filing the motion in court and seeing it all the way through until the court dissolves the marriage. Now if he refuses to settle or sign papers and I have to send registered letters to him asking him to cooperate, or if I have to negotiate with his lawyer, or if I have to make more than two appearances in court, the cost will go up. Each registered letter I send costs about $150. If he hires a lawyer and I have to negotiate a property settlement or go to court more than twice the basic cost will go up to $2500. This is why it is best if the two of you can work out your own settlement without me really having to get involved too much. To get started I need $600 minus the $20 consultation fee, so I'll need $580 before I can start to work on your motion. I'll need the balance before I can make the final motion with the court.

After a long moment of silence Sara replies that she doesn't have enough money and she is not sure what she wants to do. Sam smiles and says he understands. When she decides what she wants to do she should come back. Sam hands Sara a copy of the written estimate and says, "If you decide to pay for services in the next 48 hours I can apply the $20 consultation fee to the balance. After 48 hours have passed I can't offer you that discount."

After Sara left, Sam told me that she would definitely be back. When I asked him how he could be sure, Sam replied, "Divorce clients rarely come here and sit through the consultation unless they have already made up their minds. This one is in a bad situation with an unemployed, drinking husband and young children. She just needs to come up with the money." Indeed, less than 48 hours later Sara returned with $580 in cash. My observations and reports from lawyers confirm that it is common for divorce clients to have to return with the funds to begin services after the initial consultation. Few divorce clients know what the costs will be before the consultation. In addition, during the recession of the early 1990s, when my data were collected, few clients had easy access to $600 or more. Divorce clients are usually asked to make the first down payment in cash.

The worksheets provide attorneys with virtually all the relevant questions to ask clients. This in turn aids in the standardization of services to clients. The same information is obtained from each client about the relevant services. If client responses do not fit the categories listed on the worksheet, attorneys usually have little choice but to inform them that the firm does not handle their type of case. Phil, one of the managing attorneys introduced in Chapter 2, explains:

You have to realize . . . that the profit margin on these small items is much higher than the profit margin on major litigated cases. . . . So for us to do a will, where we are going to get 100 percent of the fee, which essentially [my secretary] does—I check off the boxes and review it, of course, but she essentially does the whole thing—is a very high profit item for us. I have found by working here, if you do a lot of very high profit items where you get 100 percent of the fee, that makes a lot more sense for this type of practice than it does to get involved in some major type of litigation.

To maintain profitable practices, attorneys who work for franchise law firms learn to emphasize the most basic services which involve the least amount of work. During Sara's divorce consultation the attorney, Sam, tells her that it is best if his role is minimized. Problems a firm's production system are not equipped to handle are usually turned away in the name of efficiency and profits. This suggests there is little reason to believe clients are receiving inadequate services. On the other hand, attorney discretion is largely limited to selling the standardized services.

The selling of services is often the longest part of initial consultations. Successful attorneys often begin the process of selling the moment the client enters the office. The combination of legal advice and sales pitch used to sell legal services is evident in the previous example of Sam and Sara. Although divorce may be an emotional topic, successful attorneys focus on what services they will perform for the cost of the service. Because divorce is the most commonly provided service at Beck & Daniels and Arthur & Nelson,[2] attorneys quickly learn not to let clients become too emotional. In jurisdictions which do not allow uncontested divorces, attorneys have a natural opening by explaining what the law requires:

> Let me begin by telling you that in this state there are no uncontested divorces. There are no irreconcilable differences. [The state] doesn't want to make it too easy. There are only four causes of action for a divorce. Let me go through them. If you have one we can talk divorce. If not, you can't have a divorce. OK? Here they are: lack of support, physical abuse, mental abuse and infidelity. Do you have any of those? Usually the easiest route is to get your husband to sign a paper admitting to infidelity. Do you think he might do that? If he will that will make everything just so much easier for all of us. Now it will also reduce the cost. So let's talk about that.

With clients who are not seeking a divorce successful lawyers use a more forceful sales approach. The following detailed example from my field notes is typical. A young couple with three children wish to obtain a will. They are speaking with Phil, the Arthur & Nelson attorney quoted earlier, who has just completed asking them questions based on the firm's worksheet for wills. Phil explains to the young couple that the firm only offers a single will, but it will suffice for their needs since their "main concern should really be just to protect their three young children in the case of a death of one or, God forbid, both of you." He explains to the couple that

> Arthur & Nelson only offers one type of will, a sort of one size fits all. What's called a simple reciprocal will. Each adult automatically leaves everything to his or her spouse in the case of death, including custody of the children. It also provides for the children to inherit their parents' estate, split equally among them, in the event both of you should die. And there are also provisions for alternate executors and guardians for the children, in case you want to name a brother and a sister or someone from both families. So, you see, this will has everything you'll ever need. In fact, what we'll give you is a copy of your wills, one for each of you, on this nice thick legal paper, and these folders to keep them in [holds up paper

and folders]. When they're complete you should look them over, and when you're satisfied that everything's OK, you should really put them in a safety deposit box or safe and not look at them again for a long, long time.

The cost of the service is approached in a similar manner. Phil opens the Arthur & Nelson pricing book to the page titled wills, turns the notebook toward the clients, and points out the charge for the basic service with his pen. He then says, "You can see for yourself what the service will cost. This covers everything you need. There are no hidden costs, no added fees later. O.K.? Can we go ahead? You really should do this. To protect your young children." After a moment of staring at each other the couple agrees. Phil continues, "to do the work I'll need a deposit of 50 percent. Bring the other half when you pick it up. Or, you can put the whole thing on Visa or Mastercard and take care of it all right now."

Not all attorneys are as aggressive as Phil. Less experienced staff attorneys appear to be less willing to tell clients what to do and tend to offer them more choices. For example, Steve, an Arthur & Nelson staff attorney, offered a client complaining of poor mechanical service on her automobile three choices, ranging from least expensive to most expensive: The client can write a letter to the dealership explaining the vehicle's problems, the mechanic's failure to repair the problem after repeated attempts, and demand that the problem be solved or her money refunded; the lawyer can write the letter to the dealership for the client; or the client could opt to take the dealership to court. But the client became distressed when Steve refused to choose the "best" option for her. She left without buying any services even though she expressed apprehension about trying to continue to deal with the dealership herself.

In another example, a client at Beck & Daniels had defaulted on a used car loan (at 48 percent interest). The creditor had already repossessed the auto and attached the client's paycheck to recover the losses. The client's main concern was to stop the creditor from taking the paycheck. The staff attorney, Chuck, explained the client's options: the attorney could negotiate a payment schedule with the creditor (for a fee of $275); the client could declare bankruptcy (for a fee of $800); or the client could simply let the creditor take the money from his wages. Chuck did not suggest any one of the options and the indecisive client did not choose to buy any services. Successful attorneys convince clients to buy their services by offering a specific course of action. While less experienced staff attorneys offer clients a list of appropriate actions, more experienced attorneys try to offer a solution. The managing attorneys I observed with clients sometimes explained the different options to their clients as did the staff attorneys. But managing attorneys more often concluded by saying "now here's what I'd like to do, . . ." "this is best handled if we move quickly to, . . ." or "I can take care of this for you by. . . ." Attorneys who are most successful convince clients that they can solve their problems—no matter what the problem is. Only a few attorneys report that they do not accept clients because they don't know how to handle their problems. Kenneth, a Beck & Daniels managing attorney makes this point while advising a new staff attorney who complained that he just had to "bullshit" through a consultation:

Never talk about advice. Never tell how you are going to do something. When you are sure you know what their problem is, tell them you can solve it. Say nothing more about it. As long as you know what their problem is you can find out what to do. There are 40 lawyers in this firm in this city. If they don't know about it, they each know twenty more lawyers. Someone knows how to take care of the problem and you can find them. Always tell the client you can solve the problem.

In practice the choices confronting attorneys are rarely as expansive as Kenneth's words suggest. Secretaries screen out almost all of the inappropriate clients before they have the opportunity to meet with an attorney. I observed over 80 consultations. Only once did a secretary allow an inappropriate client to consult with an attorney. (A woman who had been sexually harassed at work. The secretary knew the firm could not handle the case but felt the client should at least have the opportunity to tell her story—even if only for 15 minutes).[3] The choices attorneys are faced with often revolve around more technical issues. For example, finding out if a teenager can change her name without the consent of her father or determining if there are different forms for residential real estate closings in counties with Torrens rather than deed title transfer systems.

Arthur & Nelson management circulates a list of branch office attorneys claiming to have some expertise in particular areas of law. If an attorney isn't familiar with an area of law, he or she is encouraged to consult with an appropriate lawyer from the list of "experts." However, consulting the list of experts with a client sitting in the office means admitting that you don't know how to solve a client's problem. Branch office attorneys try to avoid such admissions. Consulting the list of experts appears to force attorneys to shift from marketing themselves to marketing the benefits of the firm to the client. For example, during a consultation I observed an attorney did not know if a minor could change her name without her father's consent. The father had left the family years before and the pregnant teenager wanted to change her last name to her mother's maiden name. As a single mother the teen wished to pass her mother's maiden name to her child. The teen's father had been located but refused to sign the consent form. The attorney first tried to persuade the teenager to ask her father to sign the form again. When both the teenager and her mother rejected that proposal as futile, the attorney suggested the teen should rethink her plans. "Perhaps the baby should have the benefit of the grandfather's name," she suggested. When the attorney was finally forced to admit that she did not know how to proceed, she called one of the "experts" on the firm's list. After confirming that there is a process allowing for the teenager to change her name without her father's consent, the attorney remarked,

that's the great thing about being part of such a large, nationwide law firm. There is always someone who knows the answer when you don't. That's why we have these lists of experts to consult with. It's impossible for every attorney to know everything. That's one of the reasons I really like working with Arthur & Nelson.

The Arthur & Nelson list of experts creates a number of paradoxes for the attorney. First, to use the list with a client listening is to admit that one does not know what to do for the client. Second, a number of Arthur & Nelson attorneys, including the one in the above example, complain that "a big problem here is that some of my colleagues in other offices take cases that they know nothing about because they don't want to lose part of their fee by referring it out." Yet the list of experts may encourage such behavior by helping attorneys to obtain quick answers, rather than referring the case to another attorney with more experience. Attorneys must try to balance their need to market their services with serving the client. Arthur & Nelson's list of experts is an attempt to provide attorneys with more choices when trying to balance their needs against the client's needs. The list provides a network of information for Arthur & Nelson attorneys and a last resort marketing tool (i.e., marketing the firm).

Beck & Daniels attorneys have no similar tool. Beck & Daniels attorneys rely on personal networks, both within the firm and outside of the firm, when they need additional information. One Beck & Daniels managing attorney claims that he only "gives advice, I don't get it. There is nobody in this region right now who is capable of advising me." But other Beck & Daniels attorneys speak of their personal networks when asked about needing legal advice. For example, managing attorneys such as Renee—who often are experienced attorneys when they are hired—look to friends outside of the law firm.

As far as legal questions, it depends what area and who I think would know that area best. . . . I have friends in town that have specialties or expertise in things and they are more than happy usually to give an answer.

Like Chuck, less experienced staff attorneys usually work informal networks in the firm before seeking advice from outside friends and aquaintainces:

I will go to my managing attorney; if not my managing attorney, somebody from another office that I've spoken with in the past or know has a special knowledge of a certain area. Or I will call upon one of my friends that works in that area, whether it be a public defender, a state's attorney, or somebody that works in a different office.

It appears that Beck & Daniels attorneys may not be as well prepared as their Arthur & Nelson counterparts to handle client problems they are not familiar with. However, Beck & Daniels' case menu system limits the types of cases the attorneys may handle. If attorneys turn away clients with problems not listed on the menu, they may be less likely to enter areas they are not familiar with. In any case, by dealing only with case types from the approved menu, Beck & Daniels attorneys are likely to find worksheets and computer boilerplates to fit their needs.

Attorneys from both firms report that they regularly turn clients away if they cannot afford the services or if they perceive personality conflicts with the client. For example, Arthur & Nelson's Phil explains that he trys to discourage clients he does not want to work with

in the following manner: Quote them a fee that's slightly high and unreasonable, because the clients I feel are psychologically or mentally a problem. . . . Some clients will come in and sit down and everything seems normal. Before you know it they want to sue either George Bush or [the governor]. . . . And basically you frighten them with the fees. It would be a surprise if they ever retain. However, what you do tell them is legally correct, that they could sue, there's no doubt about it, you could sue anyone in this country. The fees may be 10,000 dollars in trial and everything else. This usually deters them. Also, there are some clients I feel who are obnoxious, and either way, I more or less try to give them a higher fee quote on what their problem could be. And if they retain, at least it's worth the aggravation.

Sam, a Beck & Daniels managing attorney, is a bit more direct than Phil:

Do you ever turn clients away?
You betcha.
For what reasons?
If I think what they want me to do is really repulsive, or if for some reason they are so mentally disabled it is going to be difficult to work with I won't serve, basically on those two bases. If they don't have the money to pay, obviously, they are not my clients. But I've had people come in who were in "la la land." [I say to them] "Hey, look, here's your $20 back, I can't help you;" or, "Look, what you are planning is just, it borders on fraud, or it's simply not prudent to do. I don't want to represent you." I'll just tell them. Those are basically the only reasons why I refuse people service.

On the other hand, only a few attorneys report that they do not accept clients because they don't know how to handle their problems. This is partly because of the need to sell services to as many clients as possible to maintain profitable offices. But, as I discuss in the next section, it is also because the vast majority of clients have routine legal needs.

PROCESSING LEGAL FORMS

Attorneys employed by franchise law firms spend much of their time at the office consulting with clients to sell a limited set of services. The nature of the franchise production system demands that attorneys be present during virtually all hours branch offices are open. For example, the branch office attorneys in my sample report that in a 49-hour average work week, 36 hours (73%) are spent working at the office. The remaining time is divided between court (10 hours), other lawyers offices (.9 hours), law libraries (1.5 hours) and real estate closings (.6 hours). The small amount of time spent at law libraries (3%) suggests the routinized nature of legal work at these firms. Even this small amount of time reported for doing research at law libraries may be exaggerated. A number of attorneys report that their offices "have law libraries," meaning statute and form books, and that their library research really takes place at the office. In the following quote, Steve, the Arthur & Nelson staff attorney discussed earlier, explains why it is rarely necessary for attorneys at franchise law firms to leave the office.

For every case I do there's a case that's similar. I can look in that case and see if there's a motion in there. I can look at that motion. There's a "how to," an answer to a complaint that I need with a counter claim. There's always a case that we get that's similar to a case that we've had in the past that I can always, like, look up and check my work and see if I'm doing it right. Or if I have no idea, just to look up, just to get an idea on how to do it. That's what we [do]. Because of the high volume there's always something that we had before.

Only the time spent at court to make motions and file documents significantly detracts from the time spent at the office. Attorneys try to limit their time in court to one day a week, if possible, because "the time spent waiting to go before a judge for fifteen minutes is totally unproductive time. We don't consult with clients at the courthouse."

The incentive systems clearly reward attorneys for their sales skills. Although we might expect the sales-oriented nature of work at franchise law firms to be a source of frustration for lawyers, this is not necessarily the case. Attorneys report that selling services to clients is the most interesting and challenging part of their job. Even though the legal cases may be highly repetitive, the contingencies of human interaction make it impossible for attorneys to always follow rigid scripts when conducting consultations (see also Leidner 1993).[4]

The legal fields we practice in aren't that diversified. I think 90 percent of the time what I'm doing is either something to do with bankruptcy law or what I call DRL or FCA law—domestic relations law or [the] family court act. Very rarely do I get called on to answer a question of military law. Very rarely do I get called on to answer a question of maritime law, airplane disaster law, multimillion dollar estate planning. People just don't come to Arthur & Nelson for that. *On the other hand, the problem of every person is unique* and even if it's a type of divorce I've seen before, there's going to be one quirk that's different. Maybe three kids in this one, two kids in the last one. . . . *So even though the fields are not diversified, each person comes to me and the case is unique because each individual is unique.* . . . So in terms of fields of law, not very diversified, but I still think each case presents its own challenge, each case presents its own excitement. (emphasis added)

The "excitement" of working at franchise law firms is in the interaction with clients. In this context, a successful attorney is someone who can sell services to all types of people.

The day-to-day tasks of writing letters, filling out contracts and other documents, and going to court are more mundane tasks for attorneys at franchise law firms. One Arthur & Nelson managing attorney calls this work "processing law" instead of practicing law to denote its routine nature: "Obviously, I'm an attorney, and at Arthur & Nelson I process law. In that sense it's not diversified [work]." Attorneys at both firms echo this view of their work. From Arthur & Nelson:

I thought there would be interesting work. . . . Interesting work? I mean, sometimes it's interesting work . . . but I wouldn't say it's fascinating work. A lot of it's drudgery.

The work gets monotonous because I'm constantly doing divorces, you know, and I wish there was more of a range.

From Beck & Daniels attorneys:

Within the limitations of what a law practice is—or what the management of people is—it's varied and diversified. But it's predictably varied and predictably diversified to a point where it becomes routine and almost punch-press boring.

About 85 to 90 percent of it is the same, day in, day out. Divorce, bankruptcy, wills—that sort of stuff. Then in terms of administrative work, it's pretty much the same. . . . Ten percent of the cases I'd say are kind of out of the ordinary, but generally 90 percent of what I do, 80–90 percent, is probably pretty routine, pretty much the same.

Data from attorneys at both firms on how they spend their time working confirm the anecdotal accounts. Attorneys spend the majority of their time working on family law and bankruptcy cases. Arthur & Nelson attorneys report spending significantly more time working with family law issues (51 percent) than do Beck & Daniels attorneys (30 percent). This is best explained by the differing advertising strategies of each firm. Beck & Daniels airs very general television advertisements which state that its "neighborhood" law offices deal with a variety of legal issues and personal problems.

Arthur & Nelson, on the other hand, tends to target specific areas of practice in its advertising. Target practice areas have included an emphasis on divorce. More recently, Arthur & Nelson advertising has also targeted personal injury and bankruptcy. It is not surprising, then, that Arthur & Nelson attorneys spend the majority of their time working on divorce, personal bankruptcy and personal injury intake, while Beck & Daniels attorneys divide their time among a wider variety of case types (including family, bankruptcy, wills, criminal and real estate).[5]

These differences also make sense when one considers the organization of work and technology at each firm. Beck & Daniels' production system provides highly computerized boilerplates and form letters for seven general case types (family law, civil law,[6] wills, residential real estate, business incorporations, personal injury and criminal[7]). In branch offices these seven case types are referred to as "the menu of services." (Much like McDonald's provides a very specific and limited menu of foods to order in its stores.) It is this menu which secretaries use to screen clients.

Because Arthur & Nelson branch offices are much less dependent upon computers, the firm provides a different strategy to help secretaries and staff attorneys become proficient in constructing documents and letters. By targeting advertising to specific practice areas, Arthur & Nelson management helps to reduce the diversity of clients dealt with by branch offices. As discussed in Chapter 2, Arthur & Nelson branch office personnel increase their productivity by specializing in divorce. The other target areas are referred to specialized units within the firm where specially trained secretaries process the files. Thus, Arthur & Nelson managing attorneys often refer to themselves as divorce or family law specialists when asked to characterize their practices:

[I am a] general practitioner, specialist in matrimonial law.

I would say [I am a] specialist. I personally do only matrimonial and family law.

In contrast, all Beck & Daniels attorneys in my sample characterize themselves as general practitioners with no specialties or concentrations. Although one astute attorney does suggest that general practice at Beck & Daniels should be considered a type of specialty:

You know, it's funny. I'm a general practitioner by any definition of the law, but if you think of it, it's kind of a specialty. You're taking only a certain menu of cases, your clientele is only a certain type of people—only middle-class individuals—and you're not representing businesses or banks or anything like that. So in a way it's kind of a specialty to acknowledge. It's not a specialty you could register [with the bar association] or anything like that, but maybe it would be a calling to do this kind of work.

The limiting of case types dealt with at each firm and the routinized nature of the work allows secretaries to become virtually as "expert" as many lawyers. In fact, during interviews a few lawyers admitted to allowing secretaries to perform initial consultations during times when clients were scheduled but no lawyers were available at the office. However, the more important point for the present discussion is that the standardized production techniques of franchise law firms delegates significant legal decision-making responsibilities to secretaries.

Branch office attorneys report spending only 26 percent (9.5 hours) of their weekly office hours writing or preparing documents. Furthermore, many attorneys admit that much of the time they place in the writing and preparing categories actually belongs to secretaries who do the work for them. In the following example, Ned, a Beck & Daniels attorney hired by the firm to process a large probate case load, explains the importance of secretaries in writing letters, drafting documents and managing case files.

She evaluates the estate. She prepares the forms. She sends them out to the clients. All I do is sign the letter. When the forms come back she prepares them for filing at the court. She requests the check and writes the check. I don't even touch it. Then, if there is a hearing, I go to the hearing. When I come back I give her the order or whatever it might be. She takes it from there. . . . She types it up, sends it to the client, makes sure . . . (trails off). Then when it comes back I just hand it to her. She makes sure all the canceled checks and the receipts are there. She finds out how much court costs are due. She sends it down for filing. So if she left, I'd be dead.

Less "specialized" attorneys also admit that they delegate most writing tasks to secretaries. The first example is an Arthur & Nelson attorney, the second is from Beck & Daniels:

It's really talking to clients and consultations that is the biggest part. The rest of the work, we may only dictate two letters to the secretary or give her the form which takes [me] 15 minutes. That could be an hour's work for her. The initial consultation sheet, like when you saw me last night, [only] took me part of the [fifteen minute] consultation. That was it. I gave it to her.

Writing, drafting, dictating legal memos, briefs. . . . It's not an answerable question because we have selection modules. We don't have to do a whole lot of drafting. *We just make circles in crayon*. I probably do five hours of that a week. Preparing legal documents, that's the same thing. Five hours a week is the total for both—writing stuff and preparing documents. (emphasis added)

Beck & Daniels' consultation worksheets are organized to facilitate the use of computers. Case types are broken down into computer modules. During consultations attorneys circle the computer module numbers that respond to the client's case type. Secretaries then enter these numbers into the computer to create letters, simple wills, standard motions and pleadings, etc. from boilerplate programs. It is this process that the attorney in the above quote is referring to when he remarks that "we just make circles in crayon."

From the standpoint of mass producing legal services, limited case types and routinized production procedures mean high productivity levels with as many case files as possible opened and closed in any day, week or month. Attorneys at franchise law firms do not sell their legal expertise to clients. Rather, they use a generalized claim of legal expertise (which is largely assumed by clients) to sell prepackaged legal services. Many lawyers employed by franchise law firms openly worry that licensure and court protections of lawyers from the unauthorized practice of law are all that protect their positions. And yet it is also inappropriate to say that secretaries have been elevated to the level of legal experts by franchise law firms. The point of mass production and the franchise organization of work is to reduce task complexity to the point where no experts are necessary. Secretaries are vital to franchise law firms. They may develop expertise with the computer systems or legal forms—just as successful attorneys become expert salespeople—but they are no more legal experts than McDonald's kitchen workers are master chefs.

THE CLIENT EXPERIENCE

At the beginning of this chapter I noted that franchise law firms obtain potential clients largely through television advertising. The advertisements generally offer clients protection from a cold and complex legal system. Franchise law firms promise to help clients with their legal problems by holding their hands, being available at convenient neighborhood locations and by charging inexpensive fees. In contrast, I have shown that clients are ushered through rigidly organized systems where secretaries and lawyers work together to quickly and efficiently sell a limited menu of services.

But what of the clients? Do they obtain the services they require? Are they satisfied with the services they receive? Unfortunately, I was not able to interview clients for this study. However, my observations of lawyer, secretary and client interactions suggest numerous implications. If clients come to franchise law firms with the expectation of fast and friendly service, they are likely to find it. Secretaries make presenting a friendly face to clients a priority. The quick consultations mean that the wait to see an attorney is relatively short. (At one Arthur & Nelson office in which I observed, the managing attorney constantly worried that clients would think I was an unproductive lawyer and become upset at having to wait 15 to 30 minutes for consultations.) Surely, franchise law firms rank as well as any modern convenience for pleasant efficiency. Managements of both Arthur & Nelson and Beck & Daniels assure me that customer response cards reveal their clients to be very satisfied with this level of service.

However, if clients expect to speak with an attorney for the price of an initial consultation regardless of their intentions to buy a service or their needs, they are mistaken. Initial consultation fees are not sufficiently high to allow informative chats without the possibility of further services. For clients who have legal needs beyond the scope of the firm, secretarial screening is a benefit. Screening saves both the client and attorney time and money. But on numerous occasions I witnessed secretaries and managing attorneys ejecting people from offices (sometimes by threatening or using force) when they refused to state why they wanted to speak with an attorney—even though they had the initial consultation fee in hand. Some of these unwanted clients are alcoholics, drug addicts or homeless who may be mentally unstable or unable to pay for services beyond the consultation. But other unwanted clients are middle-income people who are unsure if they have a legal problem. These prospective clients usually want to have an intelligent discussion with a lawyer. For example, Kenneth, a Beck & Daniels managing attorney quoted earlier in the chapter, told me that I would make a terrible client because I "would want to be too involved in making decisions and options." Franchise law firms are not equipped to handle people who may want very general advice. At the very least, you have to be willing to discuss your problems with the secretary and give the impression that you are shopping for a specific service offered by the firm.

For clients, attorney consultations are often rushed. The volume practice and low consultation fees make it impossible for attorneys to spend significant amounts of time listening to tales of woe. During many of the consultations I observed, clients appeared to be surprised by the forcefulness of the sales pitch. Attorneys assure clients that they can solve their problems. Yet the consultations hardly seem long enough to convince clients of this. Many clients hesitate to commit to buying services and have to be cajoled (as we saw with Phil's simple will sales pitch). And yet if attorneys do not seem self-assured and forceful, clients may conclude they are not really getting expert advice. Recall that attorneys who provide clients with multiple options of how to proceed without recommending a course of action are less successful at selling their services. Despite de-skilling theories which predict that professionals and clients will become more equal (Haug 1977, 1975, 1973), lawyers and secretaries dominate the relationship. In many cases clients who are relatively unsophisticated consumers of legal services demand that attorneys make all decisions. Clients hesitate mainly when they are asked to pay for the services chosen by the lawyer. Most clients I observed seemed satisfied as long as attorneys assured them that they would personally solve their legal problems.

Only when attorneys made mistakes in the sales process and let clients know that they were receiving standardized services rather than personalized expert services did clients become disgruntled. Phil, the Arthur & Nelson attorney selling the simple will to a young couple I described earlier in the chapter almost lost the sale when the woman asked when the will would be ready. Phil responded, "let me see how busy the girl is. If she isn't too busy you can come back in fifteen or twenty minutes." The couple was clearly stunned. The woman exclaimed, "Tonight? That fast?" The attorney, realizing his mistake, quickly said, "Well, ahh, I guess it might take a little longer, really. How about tomorrow afternoon?"

After the couple had left Phil admitted he had made a mistake. Clients expect their legal documents to be "uniquely crafted" by trained professionals. They don't expect to pay a substantial amount of money ($350) to have a secretary construct the document on a computer in fifteen minutes. No doubt this is another reason why branch office attorneys tend to stress the individuality and challenge of each client they sell services to, rather than the repetitive procedures used to process the legal forms.

NOTES

1. This chapter is a revision of my article (Van Hoy 1995), "Selling and Processing Law: Legal Work at Franchise Law Firms," in *Law and Society Review*, 29: 703–729.

2. My sample of attorneys at both firms report that they spend most of their time consulting with clients for divorces, personal bankruptcy filings, wills and personal injury settlements. At Arthur & Nelson attorneys report spending 51 percent of their time on divorces, 17 percent on personal bankruptcy filings, 12 percent on personal injury intakes and 6 percent on wills. At Beck & Daniels the numbers are 30, 24, 5 and 19 percent, respectively.

3. While the secretaries I observed did an excellent job of screening out inappropriate clients, they did sometimes make mistakes in the coding of client cases handled by their firms. For example, during my office visits at Arthur & Nelson a client who wanted advice about declaring bankruptcy was erroneously coded as wanting a divorce.

4. Some scripts are imposed on attorneys. For example, both firms script attorney advice about the rights and responsibilities of clients seeking personal bankruptcy protection.

5. Arthur & Nelson managing attorneys spend about 84 percent of their time working on family (54.5), personal bankruptcy (21.4) and plaintiff's personal injury (7.7) cases. Staff attorneys spend about 78 percent of their time on these case types as well (47.5, 14.2, 15.8, respectively). At Beck & Daniels, family law, personal bankruptcy and plaintiff's personal injury only account for about 57 percent (29.3, 22.2, 5.0, respectively) of managing attorney efforts and 61 percent (30.0, 26.4, 4.8, respectively) of staff attorney time. Wills, criminal cases and residential real estate closings account for another 32 percent of managing attorney and 37 percent of staff attorney efforts at Beck & Daniels. However, at Arthur & Nelson wills, criminal and residential real estate work account for only 16 percent of managing attorney and 16 percent of staff attorney time.

6. Civil law includes personal bankruptcy, consumer problems and landlord-tenant disputes.

7. Beck & Daniels branch offices only complete initial consultations for personal injury and criminal cases. After the initial screening these cases are co-counseled with specialists from other law firms.

4

Franchise Law Firms and Traditional Practice

Franchise law firms occupy a well-defined niche in the market for personal legal services. Firms such as Arthur & Nelson and Beck & Daniels seek a clientele that is likely to choose a lawyer based on advertising rather than personal networks (or what is commonly called "word-of-mouth advertising"). Clients are ushered through a production system where the main goal is to sell them prepackaged services. Imbedded in this analysis is an implicit argument that the services provided by the franchise firms are qualitatively different from the services offered by more traditional personal services lawyers. Yet this is an argument that needs careful attention. The line which distinguishes the work of attorneys at franchise law firms from solo and small-firm practitioners is not completely clear. In Chapter 1 we saw that attorneys employed by the franchise firms have similar social characteristics as other personal services lawyers. In addition, much, perhaps even most, personal services law is routine and may be standardized (Carlin 1994; Heinz and Laumann 1982; Seron 1996; also see Chapter 1). For example, a solo practitioner who attended law school after first working as a CPA complains that it's easy to practice law, . . . [for example] real estate closings. Any monkey who's got a law degree and has done ten real estate closings can do real estate closings and do a very good job at it. Is it difficult law? No, because . . . first of all, it's not that mentally challenging for a solo practitioner, at least it's not for me, and I'm no rocket scientist.

In this chapter I take a more careful look at how these two types of legal practices are similar and different. Generally, it is in the organization of work, not the legal issues dealt with, that franchise law firms may be distinguished from solo and small-firm practitioners.

In the analysis that follows I present data for my samples of solo and small-firm lawyers in Chicago, and franchise lawyers. I have removed from the sample one solo practitioner who reports specializing 50 percent in patent-trademark work and 50 percent in business-corporate work. This attorney reports offering no personal legal services, making his work distinct and not comparable to other lawyers in the sample. For example, while most of the attorneys in my sample report spending an average of five to twelve hours per week preparing legal documents, this attorney reports spending twenty-one hours per week on that task. Four other solo practitioners who "specialize" in business-corporate work remain in the sample because they also offer personal legal services (mainly real estate closings and divorce services).[1] In addition to my two samples of attorneys, I compare my findings to Carlin's (1994) classic study of solo practitioners in Chicago. Seron's (1996) recently published study of the business practices of 100 solo and small-firm attorneys in New York also informs the analysis presented in this chapter.

Table 4.1 shows how my samples of 34 solo and small-firm practitioners and 43 attorneys employed by franchise law firms report spending their time during an average work week. The solo and small-firm practitioners report spending about five hours each day (or 66 percent of their total working time) at their offices. This is similar to Carlin's (1994, p. 41) findings about the work practices of solo practitioners in Chicago. Carlin's respondents spent an average of four to five hours per day in their offices.[2]

In contrast, attorneys at Arthur & Nelson and Beck & Daniels spend 72 percent of their working time (or six hours each day) at

Table 4.1
Number of Hours Traditional Practitioners and Franchise Attorneys
Report Working In and Out of the Office

	TRADITIONAL		FRANCHISE	
	Hours	**Percent**[a]	**Hours**	**Percent**[a]
Office	29.5	66	35.6	72
Court	7.0	16	10.0	20
Police Stations	0.0	0	0.025	0
Real Estate Closings	3.4	8	0.6	1
Law Library	0.6	1	1.5	3
Other Law Offices	2.6	6	0.9	2
Other	1.4	3	0.9	2
Total	**44.5**	**100**	**49.5**	**100**

[a]Percents are of total working time.

their offices. Among the franchise attorneys, only Arthur & Nelson
staff attorneys report spending as little time at the office as the solo
and small-firm practitioners (65 percent versus 66 percent of their
working times, respectively). All other franchise attorneys report
spending at least 72 percent of their working time at the office.

Solo practitioners and small-firm attorneys report spending more
time at real estate closings and at other lawyers' offices than is the
case for franchise attorneys (1 percent and 2 percent, respectively).
However, solo and small-firm lawyers spend slightly less time at
the courts than do franchise lawyers.[3] This is apparently a result
of the high-volume nature of the franchise law firm practice. As
Carlin notes (1994, p. 118, note 3), "A good part of the time in
court is apparently consumed in just 'hanging around,' waiting to
be heard on motions and pleadings or to transact business with
the clerks" (see also Chapter 3 of this volume). Attorneys working
at Arthur & Nelson and Beck & Daniels spend more time at the
courts because, as we shall see, they have more clients to file documents for. The bulk of personal legal services has little to do with
litigation. Again, Carlin's (1994, p. 118, note 3) work is instructive: "While most individual practitioners spend at least some time
in court, very few actually try cases" (see also Seron 1996, pp. 117,
121).

Table 4.2
How Traditional Practitioners and Franchise Lawyers Report Spending
Time at the Office

	TRADITIONAL		FRANCHISE	
	Hours	**Percent[c]**	**Hours**	**Percent[c]**
Reading Legal Material	2.6	9	2.8	8
Writing[a]	6.4	23	5.8	17
Preparing Legal Documents[b]	8.5	30	5.4	16
Negotiating	2.9	10	3.6	11
Talking to Clients	7.7	27	16.3	48
Total	**28.1**	**99**	**33.9**	**100**

[a]Includes writing, drafting, dictating legal memos, briefs, letters, etc.
[b]Includes contracts, leases, wills, etc.
[c]Percents are of total work time at the office.

Although attorneys at franchise law firms spend more time at
the office and at the courts, solo and small-firm practitioners spend
a much higher percentage of their time writing and preparing legal
documents. Table 4.2 provides a breakdown of how the two
groups of lawyers report spending their time at the office. Solo and
small-firm lawyers spend 23 percent of their time at the office writing, drafting and dictating letters and memos versus 16 percent for
franchise attorneys.

Furthermore, for solo and small-firm practitioners preparing legal documents takes twice the percentage of total time at the office
than is true of attorneys at franchise law firms. As expected, it is
at the office that the differences between the prepackaged service
delivery systems and traditional work organization are most apparent. Attorneys at franchise law firms spend less time creating
legal documents and letters, and spend more time selling services
to clients. Seron (1996, p. 82) has found that attorneys who work
in small firms or as solo practitioners can be placed on a continuum
of standardization and computerization in their work. "Small firms
tend to be anchored at one end by those attorneys who dictate into
a machine and have their secretaries print out boilerplate forms to
be worked over and then returned to the secretary for reentering.

At the other end are a few hold-outs who dictate to a secretary and then work from the transcription." Solo practitioners are somewhat more likely to work directly with their documents at a computer than are attorneys in small-firm arrangements.

In any case, the point for the present discussion is that personal services attorneys in traditional practice settings are more likely to *work with their documents* than are attorneys at franchise law firms. In modern personal legal services practices the issue is not whether one uses boilerplate forms, documents and letters. Rather, it is what the attorney does with the boilerplate that matters. In contrast to more traditional practitioners, attorneys at Arthur & Nelson and Beck and Daniels speak mainly of "review[ing] the documents for typographical and grammatical errors" after they have made "circles in crayon." Thus, even though solo and small-firm attorneys admit that "a lot of our work is cut and paste" (Seron 1996, p. 77), these attorneys are making decisions that are not feasible at franchise law firms.

Franchise lawyers spend almost half of their time at the office talking to clients versus less than one-third for solo practitioners and small-firm lawyers. This reflects the fact that franchise law firms provide a volume legal practice. Branch offices must sell and process a high volume of services to produce profits. Solo and small-firm practitioners hope to gain one to ten new clients a month (depending on the areas of practice they concentrate in).[4] Attorneys at Arthur & Nelson and Beck & Daniels often hope to gain that many new clients each day. None of the solo or small-firm attorneys carries more than 50 open case files. But attorneys at Arthur & Nelson and Beck & Daniels often complain of being saddled with 70 to 100 (or more) open case files at any time.

Solo and small-firm practitioners tend to charge somewhat higher fees for their services and be more selective in the clients and cases they accept than is the case for attorneys at franchise law firms. These attorneys are often highly critical of high-volume law practices and believe that they themselves provide better quality services. For example, Megan, a real estate attorney complains that

there are some attorneys that get ten, fifteen, twenty referrals a month. . . . I've dealt with some of these attorneys and you'll find that they are

never there. They have never seen the file. I have been to closings where
the attorney sees the file for the first time at the closing. . . . And there are
times when I got so frustrated with that because there [were] things that
I wanted to discuss that were legal that had to do with the quality of the
transaction . . . other than scheduling closing dates or arguing about our
tax figure.

Donald, a general practice attorney explains, using a less critical
tone:

There are some days where one file will keep you occupied most of the
day, and then there are other days when you can get to three, four, five,
six files, depending on what exactly is involved. . . . I think the more volume you have, the harder it is to devote quality time to all your files.
Luckily, I don't ever let my files get on top of me like that. I try to keep
my desk fairly clear and keep a handle on things and try to look a couple
weeks down the road and not just do it day-to-day.

Seron (1996, p. 68) also finds that most solo and small firm attorneys "do not construct organizations designed to anticipate a
volume business." Small-firm organization remains largely collegial
with an ideology that Seron describes as being familial. Close
friendships and tight fraternal bonds are the basis for decision
making in small partnerships. In fact, Seron finds that most partnerships are not founded on written contracts, but "handshake"
deals. The details of each agreement and organization of work are
negotiated and renegotiated on a regular basis.

The result is that traditional personal services attorneys organize
their practices in a manner that allows them to claim that the client
benefits from their "personal touch" or "bedside manner" (Seron
1996, p. 110). In contrast to attorneys at Beck & Daniels and Arthur & Nelson, the traditional practitioners often refer cases to
other lawyers that they cannot deal with or do not wish to deal
with. For example, David, a solo practitioner whose mainstay is
divorce, developed a regular practice of accepting, but then referring "crappy little collections cases" to small firms where associate
attorneys handle them. The result is that he is able to spend more
time working on the cases he believes are more important.

I just made the comment the other day to a lawyer that he lost a case because he didn't spend enough time on it. I mean, I didn't spend a lot of time on it, but I knew what the case was about . . . and he didn't. It was a disgrace. A lot of lawyers fly by the seat of their pants. . . . Something that has a little twist to it, you have got to know the twist.

Donald takes a more client-oriented tone to explain that even relatively simple documents require significant contact with the clients.

I have people here [in the office] on wills. It's not only important to have the basic will form on your computer. People have come in here, read their wills and said, what about this or what about that, or they had neglected to mention something to me, or I had made a mistake. Today people are really conscious about wills and living wills and powers of attorney and things of that nature.

The traditional personal services lawyers view themselves as more than just "mechanics" or "technicians" (Seron 1996, p. 110). They see themselves as providing clients with a set of high quality services that cannot be replaced with lower fees. A partner in a small firm that has a practice concentrated in divorce characterizes his practice as more than

just the pure legal relationship. I think, by and large, I develop a relationship with my clients. And it's difficult for me to delegate work because I don't think that anybody does it as well as I do. People look for more than just mechanics, somebody who can do the work. I think they look for someone to hold their hand, stroke them—and not so much be their friend, but be there when they need them.

Attorneys at franchise law firms often spend only fleeting moments with their clients. In those short encounters the attorneys try to obtain all the relevant client information and sell one or more services. In contrast, solo practitioners and small-firm attorneys see their role as including a relationship with their clients. Because few traditional personal services attorneys rely on significant advertising, they attempt to cultivate relationships that may lead to more work in the future. These relationships take time to develop. Thus, the solo practitioners and small-firm attorneys I interviewed rarely report initial consultations of less than 45 minutes. In addition, the attorneys generally build multiple office visits into their client routines. The extra visits to the attorney's office offers clients opportunities to become involved in the final product if they choose. Even more, the visits offer attorneys the opportunity to show clients they care about them by explaining the current status of their case. It is instructive to recall Phil, the Arthur & Nelson attorney discussed in Chapter 3, who almost lost a sale after telling a couple that their will would be ready in only twenty minutes. None of the solo and small-firm attorneys I interviewed had similar stories to tell. Their regular practice routines apparently preclude such an event. Even the real estate attorneys in my sample—who described their practices as "volume" businesses (see Chapter 1)—report spending at least 30 minutes getting to know their clients before turning the file over to their secretaries.

There is little evidence to suggest that the work of solo or small-firm practitioners in the personal legal services market is highly complex. The literature reviewed in Chapter 1 suggests that most personal legal services work is fairly routine. The data presented here and in Chapter 1 show that solo and small-firm lawyers regularly delegate many of their legal writing tasks to secretaries or paralegals. Indeed, it is an ironic testimonial to the routine nature of legal issues dealt with by attorneys in traditional practices and at franchise law firms that each reports spending only 1 percent and 3 percent (respectively) of his or her working time at law libraries. Moreover, only about three hours a week, or about 8 percent of time spent working at their offices, is spent reading legal material. This is true even though the reading legal material category includes research for cases, keeping up with changing laws, new laws, court decisions *and* reading or proofreading letters and documents for cases.

It does not seem likely that there is a significant difference in the complexity of legal issues dealt with by franchise law firms and lawyers in traditional practices. Rather, each type of practice is distinguished by the level of standardization and routinization employed. Solo practitioners and small-firm attorneys carry fewer clients and spend more time with them. The traditional practitioners may begin from boilerplate documents that are managed by a secretary. But that is only the first step in the process. Although they may not "craft" documents such as wills in the manner envisioned by their clients, they review the documents and make changes beyond correcting spelling errors when necessary.

The prepackaged production systems of franchise law firms do not necessarily preclude attorneys from making similar changes. However, the prepackaged approach does tend to limit the attorneys' interpretations of their roles to simply selling a service. The franchise incentive systems focus attention on sales and profits, not well-considered services. Perhaps the difference is best summed up by noting that the solo practitioners and small-firm lawyers I interviewed seemed to be aware that they were selling themselves— as competent, caring individuals—in a *relationship* with clients. Attorneys at Arthur & Nelson and Beck & Daniels sell each firm's solutions to client problems.

Despite the routine nature of personal legal services work, only four attorneys in my sample of solo and small-firm practitioners refer to their work as boring, uninteresting or not sufficiently challenging. In contrast, almost all of the franchise attorneys complain that their work is very routine, and boring. The predicament of franchise lawyers is that they must spend their working time selling services to as many clients as is possible for their branch offices to make a profit. Prepackaged law, by focusing on flat fees and high-volume services, forces attorneys at franchise law firms to accept more standardization and limitation of legal decision-making and production tasks than is the case for traditional practitioners. The political economy of franchise law firms intensifies production and limits attorney autonomy to choosing between only a few choices.

NOTES

1. Attorneys who report spending more than 30 percent of their working time in a particular area of law are considered specialists. Attorneys may be classified as specializing in more than one area of law (see Chapter 1, note 7).

2. I am assuming a six-day work week, as that is what most of my respondents report. Carlin does not specify the length of his respondents' work week.

3. Carlin (1994, p. 41) reports that his sample of solo practitioners

spent "a little over an hour a day . . . in court." Assuming a five-day work week for court, Carlin's findings are similar to the average for my sample of solo and small-firm practitioners (who report spending seven hours a week in court). Carlin does not report the amount of time his respondents spent at other lawyers' offices or real estate closings.

4. Attorneys concentrating in residential real estate and probate expect to turn over clients more swiftly than do attorneys concentrating in areas such as divorce or business-corporate work.

5

Lawyer Alienation

The nature of franchise production systems is to limit individual discretion in the work process. Workers follow a more or less rigidly defined set of tasks that require little forethought. Franchise law firms follow this same general pattern. As salespeople for prepackaged legal products, lawyers at franchise law firms are subject to the same feelings of powerlessness and boredom that permeate many mass production workplaces (see, e.g., Terkel 1972). But the issue of alienation is not as simple as boredom. Attorneys at Arthur & Nelson and Beck & Daniels interact with the production systems, clients and management in many different ways and at different levels. This chapter begins to sort out these different types of interactions and experiences to explain the levels of dissatisfaction among attorneys at franchise law firms.

WHY JOIN A FRANCHISE FIRM?

As we have seen, Arthur & Nelson and Beck & Daniels offer staff attorneys and some managing attorneys relatively low pay, long hours at the office and a legal environment where intellectual challenges are lacking. Why, then, do attorneys seek employment at such firms? Staff attorneys almost universally describe their hesitation at seeking and accepting employment from franchise firms. They are often only too aware of the "dirty" reputation these firms are burdened with in the legal profession. Brian, an Arthur & Nelson staff attorney, describes his initial concerns about the firm in the language of ambulance chasers.

It's tough because you go in there with a little bit of a preconceived idea of what they're all about because of the advertising. A lot of attorneys don't think that advertising is such a good idea; kind of a little bit derogatory to the profession. So you go in there with that idea and you're thinking, you know, are these basically just ambulance chasers?

Other Arthur & Nelson staff attorneys view their previous misgivings about the firm as a form of snobbery. But as Josh makes clear, the low status of the franchise firms among other attorneys continues to be problematic:

To be honest, at first, before I interviewed, I wasn't really sure I wanted to do it because I was kind of embarrassed.
  Why?
It's just that I was not that far out of law school, a couple of years, and you have a certain snobbish attitude. You know? They advertise on T.V. That was, you know, I was into bigger and better things. It's just that people snicker and things like that. Lawyers snicker and things like that!

Many young attorneys turn to franchise law firms despite their misgivings because they are unable to find other work and need to gain some practical experience. Those who become staff attorneys at Beck & Daniels or Arthur & Nelson are not, in general, graduates of highly prestigious law schools; nor have they graduated at the top of their law school classes. Like Steve, many who would eventually seek a position with Arthur & Nelson or Beck & Daniels "spent a lot of time trying to pass the bar examination, and once I did pass the bar . . . I decided that I was just going to do whatever I could to get a job."
  These young attorneys take their less-than-exemplary records into an overcrowded and highly competitive labor market. Apply-

ing for a position at a franchise firm is often a last-ditch effort at finding a job. Andy's experience is typical:

> At first, you know, I wasn't really too thrilled about working at a Beck & Daniels. But to be truthful, you know, I needed the money. . . . [This] area's pretty depressed job-market-wise, and you'd be surprised how many overqualified attorneys, well not overqualified, but [pause] well qualified attorneys they have. And so, well, I didn't know that at the time. But what was I . . . [trails off]. Hey, I have a family so I had to take the job. I wasn't getting, you know, many other offers.

Thus, young attorneys turn to the franchise firms after recognizing that their options for positions in the field of law are severely limited. They are often unhappy or unexcited by the prospects of working for Beck & Daniels or Arthur & Nelson but have concluded that any job is better than no job—even though they may be "kind of embarrassed to even tell my friends I ended up at" a franchise law firm.

Managing attorneys also turn to franchise law firms as a result of their experiences in the personal legal services market. But rather than turning to the franchise firms as a last resort, managing attorneys are often trying to preserve a sense of independence. Managing attorneys are generally not promoted from the ranks of staff attorneys. Instead they are hired from the ranks of experienced solo and small-firm practitioners whenever possible.[1] Solo and small-firm attorneys are most often motivated to join franchise firms as protection from the competition and hassle they experience as small-business owners. Recall Sam, the solo practitioner who came to Beck & Daniels after several years that he describes as successful. As originally quoted in Chapter 1, Sam explains his desire to be a managing attorney in relation to the market: "I lived fairly well but the net income to put in the bank was not good at all. You fight the bear for seven or eight years out there and this job doesn't look all that bad—or no job looks all that bad."

Although Sam admits that he "has no particular dislike for a regular paycheck," he argues that it is not his income of about $30,000 annually that keeps him on the job. Rather, it is the franchise organization which Sam finds enticing. Managing attorneys

maintain at least a modicum of control over the day-to-day operations of their local offices while the franchise management

deals with all that crap I would hate to have to deal with: Procurement,
client complaints, public relations and getting clients to walk in the door—
which is advertising. They do all the parts of the business that are business,
as opposed to legal, and leave us more free to do the legal.

Franchise law firms are not the first choice of employment for
managing or staff attorneys. The realities of an overcrowded labor
market and competition among attorneys for clients makes job offers from Beck & Daniels and Arthur & Nelson more appealing
than they might be otherwise. Staff attorneys who assess the franchise firms to be based on a "low-salary, sweat-shop, high-turnover
. . . run-fast-or-die philosophy" do not expect to find the work
highly satisfying. Their experiences on the job tend only to exac-
erbate their lack of commitment to the franchise firms that hire
them.

The experiences of managing attorneys are more complex. Managing attorneys seek to avoid the responsibilities and risks of operating a small business while preserving some amount of
professional independence and control. The branch office managing attorney is caught in a struggle with franchise firm management
over local autonomy and broad policy input.

ALIENATION IN THE MAKING: THE STAFF
ATTORNEY EXPERIENCE

We have already seen that staff attorneys are placed into a difficult position in the organization of the franchise law firm. Treated
mainly as overhead in branch office budgets, staff attorneys are
not expected to be experienced experts. Staff attorneys receive low
pay to work long hours performing the most routine consultations
and court appearances (see chapters 2 and 3). At a minimum they
are expected to produce enough revenue to cover the costs of their
salaries and benefits. Nonetheless, managing attorneys acknowledge that secretaries are more important to their practices than
staff attorneys. Such conditions can easily be seen as contributing
to the high rates of staff attorney turnover experienced by Arthur

& Nelson and Beck & Daniels. It is uncommon for staff attorneys to remain in their offices for more than two years. Indeed, many managing attorneys claim that virtually 100 percent of staff attorneys are replaced every two years at their firms.[2]

But staff attorneys generally anticipate the poor pay and working conditions when they apply to the franchise firms. What most frustrates these young attorneys are broken promises of the potential for compensation and career growth. As one perceptive Arthur & Nelson managing attorney explains, staff attorneys

get dissatisfied. Most of the managing attorneys don't pay very well. They work them fairly hard, so in about a year or two they get dissatisfied and leave. If they stay, the managing attorney tries to keep them, so I think [that] kind of discourages them.

Beck & Daniels' incentive system is an excellent example of the type of treatment that discourages and angers staff attorneys. The firm offers staff attorneys the opportunity to earn bonuses based on the revenue they generate by selling services to clients. If staff attorneys are enticed to accept low starting salaries with the promise of bonuses, they quickly learn that it is not a sure thing. Brad, a former staff attorney complains that he earned only

$24,000 a year. That's what they started me at and that's what I ended up at. I didn't get any bonuses, contrary to what we were led to believe— bonuses were just ripe for the picking—but none were forthcoming.

Other staff attorneys complain that their bonus earnings are minimal at best. Howard had been working for Beck & Daniels for fourteen months when he remarked:

I've only drawn in a few hundred bucks [of bonus]. It's not 27 percent of all [sales revenues]. You have to go over $8700 first. You only get that little extra check. Now you got to go like, you know, if you go ten grand [in sales revenue each month], you're only going to get less than 500 bucks.

Even a managing attorney told a story about not making bonuses as a staff attorney.

When I started at Beck & Daniels . . . [my managing attorney] talked the regional manager into doing a kind of office bonus whereby she saw just about all of the clients. She was very good at getting retained. We didn't work at all with her personal [account] number. If the office made money we were supposed to split it. Found out later how Beck & Daniels works. Every month I made on my own number hardly anything. I was getting in the hole. She was amassing a huge amount of revenue. She was getting bonuses that myself and the other staff attorney never saw. When [a new managing attorney] got here, it was the first time I made a bonus. I had been there a year already.

The difficulties of attaining Beck & Daniels' promise of increasing bonuses as a reward for high sales revenues also appears to engender competition between attorneys sharing the same offices. I asked attorneys at both firms if there is competition from other attorneys in getting business. Arthur & Nelson attorneys responded by discussing solo and small-firm practitioners. But at Beck & Daniels attorneys spoke of competition within their offices. For example, Sam proudly proclaimed that

my client base, as you can see from the figures I gave you, . . . is probably three times the size *of my nearest competitor in the office*. [emphasis added]

Jake, another managing attorney, explains that since the introduction of the bonus incentive system several years ago,

I find that the attorneys are more carefully looking at the book to see that they are getting their fair share of the twelves, which are divorces, and the thirties, which are bankruptcies, that type of thing, just to make sure, because everybody's bonus depends on their revenues for the month. You have to see a certain number of the type, of case types, where the people are going to retain you in order to make your share of the money.

The Beck & Daniels incentive system encourages attorneys to compete for revenue and bonuses, but the competition is not equal (as the above stories about bonuses suggest). As branch office supervisors, managing attorneys are able to disregard the formal production system to limit or prevent staff attorney bonuses. They also have incentive to do so when office profits are marginal, because staff attorney bonuses are part of the managing attorney's over-head. Some managing attorneys attempt to control labor costs by demanding to personally perform the majority of initial consultations to ensure that they sell services to the highest number of clients. Another strategy is to send staff attorneys on tasks outside of the office (e.g., to file papers in court) as they approach the revenue cut-off for earning a bonus.

Even successful managing attorneys acknowledge "that what managers have found in this firm [is] that there's not really much they can do to motivate staff attorneys." A small number of managing attorneys with highly profitable offices try to provide incentives beyond those offered by the firm to keep their staff attorneys and secretaries from quitting. Renee distributes a portion of her bonus to staff attorneys as a token of appreciation.

In fact, I share my bonus with them because I don't think they get enough from the office bonus. So out of the money I make—I've devised a formula—I give them 2.5 percent of the money I make. Then I take out taxes because I have to pay income taxes. But I let them see the numbers so they know that they are making money out of this too, because I think that's fair.

Jane motivates her branch office staff by offering gifts when short-term goals are met.

I set goals for them . . . in regard to, you know, morale and spirit and helping to increase the amount of revenues and clients we see. Like, I give Beth [my secretary] bonuses, like one month I bought her a bike because she met her goal, and one month I bought her a painting. And this month if she meets her goal she'll get something else, you know? I pay my attorneys' bonuses too. I think if you're—you have to treat your staff good in order for them to treat you [well]. And if they're happy where they work, they're going to make things good for you.

Other managing attorneys offer their staffs the opportunity to take paid personal days without reporting it to management as a sick day or vacation day.[3] Such incentives are necessary because in offices that are very profitable the base salary is kept low. In offices that are less profitable, a bonus may seem like a prize always out of reach because, as a regional manager commented, "everybody is fighting for a pie that . . . no one can really get."

Staff attorneys at both Arthur & Nelson and Beck & Daniels rapidly learn that one does not "make out" in their position. The hard work, low salary, exclusion from earning bonuses and exclusion from decision-making processes teach staff attorneys that they have little value in the eyes of firm management. Most staff attorneys believe they only have two options: Become a managing attorney or leave the firm. As Rick, an Arthur & Nelson staff attorney, succinctly puts it,

> if they're not going to offer you a managing attorney position, then why would you stay here? 'Cause you don't make very much money working for somebody else in this firm. The only way you would get any sense of making a lot of money is being a managing attorney. Not a lot, but to live comfortably, anyway.

Limited opportunities to move into managing attorney positions undoubtedly means many staff attorneys will eventually seek opportunities elsewhere. Only a few staff attorneys express an interest in managing their own offices. The others hope to gain a broad range of experience and then move on to a more specialized practice or solo practice.

The Short Career Ladder

Ideally, attorneys should be able to start at the staff level and advance through numerous career steps within each firm. Arthur & Nelson management characterizes the career path for attorneys as having three distinct steps that are similar to traditional law firms: staff attorney, managing attorney and partnership. Managing attorneys such as Phil often acknowledge this ideal career path when discussing opportunities for advancement in the firm.

> Usually one is hired as a staff attorney and if you prove your mettle, they'll eventually make you a managing attorney in a small office and then sometimes a bigger office.

Beck & Daniels potentially provides lawyers with a greater number of career paths because it is organized more like a corporation than the traditional law firm. Beyond earning bonuses, successful staff attorneys may eventually be offered managing attorney positions. Managing attorneys who successfully motivate their office staffs and maintain profitable offices may be promoted to regional managers. Finally, regional managers may eventually become national managers. Sam explains the ideal possibilities:

You can either just become a damn good lawyer working for somebody else and be very successful that way; you can be successful running your own law office as an employee of a corporation; or you can be successful as a high-level executive in the corporation.

Yet the evidence suggests that the ideal is not often obtained by either firm. The ideology of promotions and career paths is invoked to motivate young attorneys to accept job offers and work hard. But the reality is that staff attorneys rarely have the opportunity to move into managing attorney positions. By all accounts, experienced attorneys are hired to fill managing attorney positions more often than associate attorneys are promoted to those positions. After stating the Arthur & Nelson policy, Phil goes on to explain the reality experienced by most attorneys.

What happens oftentimes is, when they lose a managing attorney, and they don't have anybody in position to become a managing attorney from being a staff attorney, they sometimes hire people directly into being a managing attorney if they have any kind of experience. And then once you're managing attorney, depending on how you do and whether you're successful, they consider making you a partner.

Tom, an Arthur & Nelson managing attorney who was promoted from a staff attorney position, provides an example of how the firm actively avoids promoting its staff attorneys.

I lucked out. They looked for somebody to take over this office for many months [and] couldn't find one, so they kind of had, I kind of had it thrust upon me. But it seems to me that most of the people are hired as managing attorneys; sort of hired at the position at which they're going to remain.

Another managing attorney notes that his staff attorneys have never been promoted

because it's a limited area where you can move up in the firm. Since most of the offices are doing okay there's no need for another managing attorney there. So most of them get a lot of experience and then always a friendly parting. I mean, they make the decision where they've gotten another job, [and] where they want to specialize. The last two have gone to firms where they specialize in two areas that they were doing here which they preferred to specialize in, and they would certainly make more money.

In fact, only two of the Arthur & Nelson managing attorneys I interviewed started as staff attorneys. One cynically claimed "the person above you better be incompetent" for a staff attorney to gain a promotion.

At Beck & Daniels it is more common for staff attorneys to be promoted to managing attorney positions. However, the two reasons for this are not very encouraging for young attorneys. First, experienced attorneys who are slated to become managing attorneys are required to work for limited periods of time in the staff attorney position. These managing attorney positions are not open to the majority of staff attorneys. Second, because managing attorney turnover is almost as high as staff attorney turnover, the firm is sometimes forced to promote staff attorneys to office manager positions. (For example, Sam claims that after a two-year tenure he is now the most senior employee in his region.)

Staff attorneys who consistently generate high revenues may be asked to supervise offices. Because all managing attorneys at Beck & Daniels begin in the staff position, the criteria for promotion are universally known:

If you are a staff attorney you rise through the ranks by your revenues compared to the number of people you've seen. It's nice if you have a staff attorney who makes $10,000 every month, but it's not nice if that attorney is making $10,000 in seeing a hundred people. It's important both to see a lot of people and to actually have a high ratio of dollars per people seen. If you do that and you do it consistently . . . and the feedback from your clients is positive, then you are looked at very carefully as a potential managing attorney.

Of course, not all managing attorneys agree that an attorney's ability to generate revenue is the best criterion for promotion.

> I suppose most frequently [promotion] is based on revenue, because if you make a lot of revenue then the regional managers and the national managers will cultivate you. So you become friendly with them and after a while you can't do anything wrong. They need a managing attorney somewhere and you are put in the position. Whether or not you are qualified to be a manager is sometimes very doubtful.

In any case, the criterion of revenue generation—which is gauged by the bonuses staff attorneys earn—eliminates most staff attorneys from promotion consideration. With the incentive system operating clearly in the managing attorney's best interest, staff attorneys most often seek employment elsewhere before they are offered a promotion.

Arthur & Nelson and Beck & Daniels offer staff attorneys a trade-off. In return for initially accepting low wages and working hard, the firms offer the specter of advancement. Newly hired staff attorneys do accept the career paths offered as an incentive to work hard. However, they also quickly learn that each firm's career ladder is highly exclusive. Because they rarely see (or hear of) success stories, they correctly interpret their position as a dead end. Staff attorneys become most alienated with the franchise environment when they realize their firm's promises of advancement are mainly exhortations to work hard. From this perspective staff attorneys begin to see themselves as exploited workers—rather than professionals in training—who have little, if any, value to the firm.[4]

THE POLITICS OF LOCAL CONTROL: THE MANAGING ATTORNEY EXPERIENCE

The issue of career is defined differently for managing attorneys than for staff attorneys. It is obvious to all that management positions above managing attorney are limited and require an attorney to give up the practice of law. Most managing attorneys reasonably define advancement as earning greater compensation and developing more autonomy from management. From their vantage point managing attorneys at both firms realize that you don't rise through the ranks. You're either a staff attorney or a managing attorney. Realistically speaking, you are not going to get any higher than that.

For managing attorneys work satisfaction is based on their relationship with management. Managing attorneys often view their interests as being in opposition with firm management at the national level. But branch offices are not operated by managing attorneys (and secretaries) alone. Managing attorneys rely upon firm management to help ensure that their offices will have clients and generate revenue.

The franchise administrative offices provide a number of services to help ensure the smooth (and profitable) operation of branch offices. These include advertising, accounting and bookkeeping services, dispersal of funds to pay office expenses, help with hiring office staff, providing temporary staff to cover offices during sickness or vacations, negotiating office rental agreements and general advice about the operation of offices and legal matters. A Beck & Daniels national manager explains that

the firm provides these services so that attorneys may focus on client relations with little else to worry about: Office managers are firstly attorneys working with a case load. They are responsible for making sure the office is open and for the people under them. *We take care of everything else.* They do not recruit; they are consulted and may interview the person hired, probably as a third or second interview. [The main office] has a bureau that takes care of bookkeeping and pays the leases and such. There is a bureau they contact when fixing is needed. We take care of advertising nationally. All the attorneys have to do is take care of the clients' needs. [emphasis added]

However, managing attorneys at both firms try to minimize the role management plays in the running of branch offices. Arthur & Nelson's Keith offers a typical answer to the question: What does the main office do for the local offices?

Very little. They do the advertising. Supposedly, they sort of assist in the management of the office. They do the advertising, they do the general accounting work for the firm, and I don't know. I'd be a little hard-pressed to think what else they do. They do some hiring for the branch offices but you're generally better off if you do your own hiring.

When pressed, managing attorneys give management credit for a number of services. Nonetheless, the majority of branch office managers agree with the statement: "most of what they do for us is advertising, though." A deep distrust belies the managing attorneys' grudging acknowledgment of the important services rendered by management. Like Beck & Daniels' Frank, branch office managers "think in terms of negatives. [They] tell us what we can't do." Eric complains that Beck & Daniels' management

wastes a lot of time sending us forms to be filled out to report things that the computer could report for us in seconds. But that would take a little bit of interpretation on the part of the main office; and so they waste our time [with] filling out the forms, which just moves the information around and puts it in different squares, because they are used to working with that form. They aggravate the hell out of everybody here because they firmly believe that we are the laziest bunch of people in the world. They are trying to whip us into getting another $1,000 a month out of the public. They provide us with a paycheck, that's about all they do for us.

The national level managements of Beck & Daniels and Arthur & Nelson decide the broad issues of business direction, technology usage and advertising emphasis with little input from managing attorneys and other branch office staff. These decisions determine the types of clients and legal cases that are drawn into branch offices, how clients are served and the level of autonomy experienced by branch office staff. On one hand, managing attorneys often argue that they should be left alone to practice law and make money for their firms. On the other hand, managing attorneys are frustrated that they are not consulted when decisions are made that affect their offices. Keith, one of the Arthur & Nelson managing attorneys quoted earlier, provides a typical perspective on how policy is determined for the firm.

I have very limited input in terms of this law firm on what happens.
Why?
I have limited input because the people who make the decisions in this law firm are [the owning partners]. Also . . . the regional director, it is my

understanding, has a great deal of direct say, although not as much as the three I mentioned before. Unless you're one of those people you're not calling the shots around here in terms of where the firm is going in a broad sense.

At Beck & Daniels, managing attorneys have the same basic experience with the franchise organization.

I need to be able to say how I feel about what's going on in my office. . . . On technology I give input all the time—we need a better computer, we need this—no one listens. On budget, the issue I think really that all of the managers give that definitely the regional manager is responsive to is the fee structure—what we're charging, whether it's competitive, whether it's adequate for the amount of work required in the case—definitely they listen to what we have to say about that. But as to how the money is spent, that we don't have a lot of control over.

Managing attorneys must rely on management to guide the firm in a manner that will benefit both parties. A shift in advertising, for example, could hurt the managing attorney while increasing the firm's revenues. For example, Arthur & Nelson branch office managers became outraged when the firm budgeted "something like nine million dollars this year on personal injury ads across the country, and I don't know if they're going to spend 20 percent of that on divorce." As management decides to emphasize personal injury clients and neglect divorce, managing attorney compensation will likely decline. The firm, however, may benefit by emphasizing its special units which efficiently process the most lucrative cases.[5]

In response, managing attorneys attempt to keep as much control over their work environment as is possible. This is most evident in relations with office staff. For example, managing attorneys negotiate with management over the hiring of secretaries. Secretaries must be acceptable to both managing attorneys and management because they perform so many essential tasks. Secretaries are often a conduit between branch offices and the administrative offices. At the branch office level secretaries have contact with administrative personnel when ordering supplies, calling in the daily stats and performing basic trouble-shooting for the office. At the administrative level the firm can exert some control over the direction of the case types booked into the branch offices by offering incentives to secretaries. By maintaining a management structure for secretaries that is separate from managing attorneys, the firm divides secretarial interests. Not only do their managing attorneys evaluate them, the secretarial staff supervisors make office checks. At Arthur & Nelson, secretary paychecks are usually a combination of salary and bonus paid by the managing attorney. But they may also benefit from bonuses paid by Arthur & Nelson management separately from the managing attorney.

For example, the firm is currently offering incentives directly to secretaries for booking personal injury cases into their branch offices. This strategy helps ensure the viability of the special units despite the growing objection of many managing attorneys to the firm's increasing emphasis on them. The firm requires criminal, bankruptcy and personal injury case files to be sent to their respective special units. For these case types branch office attorney discretion is curtailed (criminal, bankruptcy) or eliminated (personal injury). Attorneys in branch offices are forbidden to make decisions on the merits of personal injury cases and advising clients accordingly. All decisions are made by staff at the special unit. Furthermore, managing attorneys must now split fees with the special units as well as firm management. It is easy to see why attorneys in branch offices might wish to avoid allocating too much of their time to doing intake interviews for cases to be sent out of the office. Secretaries, on the other hand, are eager to increase their incomes from incentives related to special units. For example, during an office visit a secretary suggested to me that many of the personal injury cases she was booking into the office "will be nothing. But if they want to pay me $16 for each one, I'll bring them all in."

What can managing attorneys do to counter the influence of firm incentives to secretaries? Very little. The most common response appears to be to delegate special unit intake work to staff attorneys. Other managing attorneys try to gain the favor of secretaries by acting as advocates for them during evaluations. By giving secretaries high marks at evaluation time and recommending pay raises, managing attorneys develop goodwill. Managing attorneys, secretaries and staff attorneys all acknowledge that staff evaluations are nothing more than administrative paper work. Neither the managing attorneys nor the staff being evaluated place much emphasis on the evaluation process. Neither secretaries nor managing attorneys could even remember the evaluation criteria. Both Ira (a managing attorney) and Stacey (a secretary) are blunt when describing the instrumental uses of staff evaluations.

We want them to have their raises in salary and we have things to fill out about how they're outstanding, good, bad, indifferent. I don't know, I can't remember whatever it is. . . . I must say that usually in the things that I've filled out I give my secretaries top rankings.

There's just like eight or nine questions that they ask: your efficiency, how dependable you are. You just have to show that form up to [management] so that they approve your increase in pay.

It is this strategy of both managing attorneys and upper management seeking to co-opt secretaries that helps keep their salaries relatively high when compared with staff attorney salaries. Because managing attorneys pay the bulk of staff salaries as part of their office expenses (and offer only positive evaluations), raises tend to be approved by firm management on a routine basis.

The administrative office has input into what salary my secretary will receive for the following year, but as a practical matter I'm paying the bills. So as a practical matter, if I suggest that she get a 5 percent wage increase or a 7 percent wage increase, they're going to give it to her.

The struggle over firm policy can be played out through secretaries only when offices are turning a profit on a regular basis. Offices that are struggling financially may not have the leverage to contest Arthur & Nelson management decisions in the same manner as their more successful counterparts. Hank, a managing attorney struggling to make his office more profitable, complains that

staffing is a function of numbers. . . . Most offices are only open two nights a week and I'm open four, but I do not have a secretary at night and that's a decision that the firm makes. I really can't override that. It's been brought up in the past but there comes a point in time when there's really no point in bringing that up.

Gerald, in another office that appears to be only marginally profitable, goes into more detail about his lack of control:

There is no input at all. I have no decision as to the location of the office, for example. We are moving. Nobody told me we are moving. I found out from the movers. People get hired and fired that I am supposed to be in charge of. Nobody tells me about that either! That's basic policy! All the decisions are made in [the administrative offices], there is no input of any substance. . . . You're like a puppet and they pull all the strings and expect you to be responsible for everything.

When a branch office is not consistently profitable the managing attorney's negotiating position with management over control within that office is diminished. Management exerts control over hiring, salary, raises and even where an office is located in an attempt to force overhead costs down. The two managing attorneys quoted above, however, are quick to point out that their offices are only marginal in the firm's accounting system. If the firm's percentage of gross revenue is counted with the managing attorney's percentage the offices are profitable. For this reason these managing attorneys believe they should have authority to hire staff to help in their efforts to increase office profit. Given the importance of secretaries for office productivity, control over hiring and raises is not inconsequential.

Beck & Daniels managing attorneys are faced with a similar set of constraints imposed on branch offices by management. Many managing attorneys describe management as controlling and limiting rather than helpful or unobtrusive. For example, managing attorneys have little say in determining the number of staff attorneys and secretaries assigned to their offices. Beck & Daniels management reserves these decisions because they take a systems approach to managing the firm. That is, management believes the production systems developed by Beck & Daniels are so unique that staffing decisions must be made above the branch office level. The national manager quoted earlier explains that

regional managers mainly recruit and train lawyers and secretaries. Because of the nature of regions and the need to match openings with applications, this is something that you would need to have taken care of at

the regional level. The same for training. The training of how to file forms
and all is unique to us, so it is something that you would want taken care
of at this level, rather than allowing office managers to teach just what
they think is important.

But regional control over staffing presents local managing attorneys with a dilemma when trying to control overhead costs. Staff
salaries are the largest portion of managing attorney overhead costs
and an important determinant of whether an office is profitable.
Another national manager explains the importance of proper office
staffing levels and the limits of managing attorney authority:

Well, one of the things for the bonus system to work . . . and really one
crucial factor . . . is having proper staffing levels for each office in the region; and as a managing attorney, making sure that the staffing levels are
correct within your office. I think that there is a tendency on the part of
managing attorneys lots of times to have too many people on staff, and
that does spread things too thin.
  Do managing attorneys make that decision?
  Well, not in most regions. Not directly, no. They sometimes will make
that decision, depending upon their regional manager; they would make
that decision about their clerical staff but usually not for the attorneys.

Although branch office staffing levels are the formal domain of
regional managers, these middle-level executives complain they are
limited by production system requirements that are imposed by
management at the national level. Max left his position as a regional manager because

there was almost a given staffing level for offices that you had to maintain.
And sometimes you thought that [an office] should go down to, you know,
from a three to a two [attorney office], but you know, it was not. You
could do it, but you were going to take a lot of grief over it as to why
you were doing that and things like that.

Indeed, the Beck & Daniels production system virtually requires
a minimum of two secretaries in each office and staff attorney hiring is guided by a theory articulated by Max as, "if you add another attorney your [client] demand increases" (see Chapter 2).
  In the section on staff attorneys I discussed how the bonus sys-

tem may foster competition between attorneys, especially managing attorneys and staff attorneys in less profitable offices. The Beck & Daniels incentive systems also may lead to tension between management and branch offices. This is because regional manager compensation is based upon a region's overall profitability. Larry, another former regional manager, explains the incentives:

Bonus was based on the profitability of a region and so it was a percentage of what that was. It's kind of a complex plan. We also had a, what we called a delta system where, if a region was losing money but was losing less than it did the year before, you got a bonus based on that. And I, really, to be honest with you, although I've only been away from it for two months, I don't even remember how we did that because it was real confusing. I mean it was, well, you know, you'd look at last year's losses and compare this year's losses and extrapolate what they were for the year and all. I mean you'd get a big form. It was about two pages long and it explained it out to you.

Regional managers are rewarded for the profits generated by branch offices under their management. But, like managing attorneys who cannot control office expenses, regional managers often find they are unable to control costs at the regional level. Larry continues,

you know, we maintained offices that should have been shut down because demographically they had changed or they should have never been put where they were in the first place. And, you know, as a regional manager, especially, you know, you have seven offices, five are profitable, and you'll find that, you know, two that were just draining the region out totally from all its revenue and we wouldn't shut them down, you know, we kept them open. And to that extent you couldn't, you were powerless to handle that problem. You knew that office should go. You knew it wasn't going to make money. You knew in your own mind it wasn't worth keeping. Yet every month you had to keep it open, every month you had to keep it staffed and every month you lost sometimes tens of thousands of dollars on an office that you realized should be shut down. And, I think, you know, a lot of the stuff, again, as a regional manager you had a certain amount of authority but you didn't have enough authority to do that.

Unable to effect long-term changes in the number of branch offices kept open or in staffing levels, regional managers are forced to look elsewhere to increase their regions' profits. Just as managing attorneys may seek to limit staff attorney bonuses, regional managers may seek to limit managing attorney compensation. While regional managers may have difficulty reducing staff levels, the Beck & Daniels production and incentive systems encourage increasing staff levels. By adding staff to branch offices regional managers can increase managing attorney overhead, lowering managing attorney bonuses. If a new staff attorney is hired the managing attorney is also forced to pay higher "black box" office costs to the firm.[6] Managing attorneys in struggling offices, such as Sam who has three staff attorneys, complain that

> when it looks like the office is going to make a profit, they stick another employee in here to reduce my net profit by increasing my salary [overhead] so that I wind up working these hours and doing this work for negative bonus at the end of the quarter.

By adding new employees to branch offices at the end of a quarter, regional managers apparently gain a more profitable region by increasing managing attorney black box payments and thwarting their attempts to earn bonuses. If branch office employment were stable this tactic would be dangerous. Eventually, labor costs would make it impossible for offices to turn a profit. Regional managers bank on their knowledge of staff attorney turnover patterns when they "suddenly" decide to add another attorney to a struggling office. From the perspective of national managers the regional manager's approach to staffing is quite irrational.

> If you've talked to anybody about the employee turnover in some of our regions, they've developed kind of a mentality that they have to have extra lawyers stacked up like fire wood in the back room in case one quits. And you know, unfortunately, you have to pay those people.

In such an environment regional managers may allow attrition to temporarily lower labor expenses. When an office becomes sufficiently profitable that managing attorneys earn bonuses, the regional partner may legitimately claim they need to replace the missing employee. Such tactics continue the firm's policy of overstaffing at the managing attorney's expense and make it difficult to reform marginal or unprofitable offices and regions. As the managing partner for Beck & Daniels points out, "it's not 50 percent of the people in all of our regions make bonus money and 50 percent don't. More often it's 75, 80 percent do or 75, 80 percent don't."

Branch office managers are engaged in constant battles with franchise firm national management over the operation and profitability of their offices. The constant negotiations with upper-level management reminds managing attorneys that they are employees rather than autonomous entrepreneurs. The result has been rising dissatisfaction and defection of managing attorneys. But in contrast to the treatment of staff attorneys as disposable, the franchise firms have sought to find career options that will keep the best managing attorneys in their offices.

Partnership: The Final Reward

Arthur & Nelson and Beck & Daniels have both developed partnership options as a reward for managing attorneys whose offices generate high profits over an extended period of time. The objective of the partner title at Arthur & Nelson and local partnership at Beck & Daniels is to keep attorneys in their offices. Phil, one of the first managing attorney partners in the Arthur & Nelson program, makes this orientation clear:

> That gets us into the question of what it means to rise through the ranks. The way you do that is you build up an office and you get a staff attorney to help you and then become your "partner." *The object is to stay in your office and work, make money, then you build the office up. You bring in extra staff people and attorneys and you make more money.* Then they eventually reward you by making you a partner. [emphasis added]

Arthur & Nelson partnership, however, is not ownership. Partners describe it as similar to company profit-sharing programs where the benefit, or monthly draw, is relatively small. Moreover, partnership at Arthur & Nelson does not significantly alter the nature of work performed by an attorney or give one a louder voice in firm policy.

I started as a managing attorney and I think there is nowhere for me to go other than becoming a partner. What that really signifies is that your compensation is higher, but in terms of your work assignments it's exactly the same. Partnership at Arthur & Nelson is a very loose concept and doesn't mean much. . . . As far as I understand it you're a partner in name only and they give you a small monthly income and that's it. . . . All I got was $100 a month, which was a token payment.

The main benefit conveyed by partnership appears to be recognition by the firm. The owning partners recognize that managing attorneys have become productive assets by awarding partnerships. Thus, managing attorneys universally report that one becomes a partner "if you just like retain tons and tons of clients and make tons and tons of money."

What many managing attorneys may not realize is that partnership also recognizes branch office autonomy for those who are making high profits. Partners are no longer supervised by district managers. By formally recognizing what was already the case for successful managing attorneys, the firm is able to eliminate a layer of management. Successful managing attorneys report that they hire staff and determine salary increases with little worry that management will interfere. Partnership formally recognizes this relationship between managing attorneys and firm management. For example, recall that successful managing attorneys often report they are not evaluated. Partners, however, report that "no one *can* evaluate my work." Thus, the true reward of partnership is that it removes direct supervision from branch offices. This allows managing attorneys who have proven that they will follow the production system the modicum of autonomy they had hoped for when they joined the firm.

The partnership program has also been instituted at the same time that Arthur & Nelson management has begun to emphasize special units instead of branch offices. The fear among branch office managing attorneys is that, as firm management shifts advertising emphasis to personal injury (and bankruptcy), they will be reduced to only intake workers for the special units. For managing attorneys to earn high compensation in the Arthur & Nelson incentive system they must process the cases at their own branch offices. Because managing attorneys depend almost exclusively on family law to keep their offices profitable, the shift away from divorce advertising is a real threat to their ability to earn significant income.

Although only a few branch office attorneys suggest that the firm "would replace us with paralegals if they could," a growing number believe they have been betrayed by Arthur & Nelson management. Because many Arthur & Nelson attorneys now consider themselves matrimonial specialists, some branch office attorneys believe they will have to find new jobs to continue to practice law and earn a living wage. The options available to branch office attorneys appear limited. They can cast their lot with the firm and hope that their loyalty is rewarded or they can leave the firm. What many attorneys admit they cannot do, however, is practice in the special unit areas they have been excluded from. After years of focusing on a limited number of case types, they no longer believe they are competent to practice in other areas.

My concern is that even though I may want to be doing this [personal injury] work . . . it's been a long time since I've really done that. And given what's at stake in personal injury cases, you really wouldn't want somebody representing clients who was not fairly well trained and recently experienced in those areas.

In response to the uncertain environment for branch office managers, the new partners have asked top management for a larger role in making decisions about the firm. It is possible that partners may become advocates for the interests of branch office managing attorneys.

On the other hand, there are signs that partners are being co-opted. Partners have been assured that they will benefit from the firm's reorientation toward personal injury and bankruptcy, even if other managing attorneys lose out to the special units. Again, Phil explains:

I think their commitment to personal injury now is important because that's a big part of the firm receiving in the future some huge sums of income. And I feel as a partner, that although that commitment to personal injury may somewhat detract from the general practice that I have, I hope—and they've led us to believe, and I think it will come to pass—

that we will be able to share, as partners, in the additional income growth of the PI [personal injury] unit. So, for example, to put it simply, if I lose $10,000 a year in salary because my family law practice is off because the advertising is after PI, but I get back $20,000 because of the PI, I have that gain of ten. So we have to go with the tide. I think there's no other way. And, basically, the decisions are made by [the owning partners] and they feel they want the firm to be committed to more of a PI structure.

The Arthur & Nelson partnership program, then, is a mechanism for rewarding and co-opting the most productive managing attorneys. The potential for high productivity, low overhead costs and lucrative settlements makes it seem likely that Arthur & Nelson will continue to reorient toward the highly centralized and routinized production process of special units (see Chapter 2). However, questions remain about how much of the proceeds from the special units management is willing to share with branch offices. At one extreme, branch office attorneys would be reduced to nothing more than intake workers for the special units. In this case, branch office attorney responsibilities and power would be significantly reduced. As intake workers, attorneys might become hourly wage-earning employees with significantly lower incomes.

Local partnership at Beck & Daniels is also oriented toward keeping successful managing attorneys in branch offices. In a similar vein to managing attorney partners at Arthur & Nelson, local partners gain responsibility for day-to-day operations at their branch offices. In fact, Beck & Daniels goes one step further than Arthur & Nelson by offering ownership equity in the firm (see Chapter 2). Beck & Daniels management hopes that if it gives branch office managing attorneys a stake in the firm they will be more motivated to increase office productivity and profits. Local partnership moves responsibility for controlling overhead costs from management to the branch offices. Local partners must directly pay their own rent, utilities, equipment, supplies, malpractice insurance and labor costs (rather than paying into the amorphous black box).

Again, similar to managing attorney partners, local partners finally gain some measure of control over salaries, incentives and staffing levels. Ending the bonus plan is one of the first changes all local partners implement. Matt, a managing attorney who recently became a local partner, provides an example of the high level of dissatisfaction all attorneys have with the Beck & Daniels bonus system.

> I have a lot of mixed feelings about the Beck & Daniels incentive system. From the way they were . . . on paper and the way they were in reality. How rules got changed and it took you two years in the firm to even figure out what the shit was they were talking about half of the time. I don't know. Under the old system, the way they paid bonus, by the time you actually got a check it was to reward you for an act that happened so far back that you didn't even remember what it was for. And I don't think that's any way to run an incentive program! [When] somebody performs you ought to give them a reward within a time frame that they are actually going to realize that it was for specific acts. Whereas before, by the time they were done jacking things around, it could be three to five months.

Even the most successful managing attorneys (who have now become local partners) have contempt for the Beck & Daniels incentive system. They refer to it as "demotivating," "thoroughly frustrating, extremely frustrating," and "just a game." Many local partners interpret their new limited authority as similar to being small entrepreneurs. But the price of this "autonomy" is an expensive equity buy-in and restrictive partnership contracts that require local partners to maintain all other aspects of the Beck & Daniels production system, including the staffing policies.

In contrast to the swift eradication of the bonus plan, only one local partner has reduced the number of attorneys and secretaries employed at his branch offices. Management's insistence that its production techniques are efficient and profitable may deter some local partners from eliminating excess production capacity. Indeed, if local partners continue to accept management's approach to staffing branch offices, they may continue to be hampered by excessive labor costs despite otherwise efficient production systems.

The franchise work environment creates dissatisfaction and disaffection among attorneys at many different levels. Staff attorneys recognize their roles as exploited laborers in a routinized production process only after realizing that they have been misled by management. Their labor market position forces staff attorneys to accept positions that require long hours of routine work with minimal compensation. But it is the setting of unachievable goals and incentives by the franchise firms that leads staff attorneys to the conclusion that they are virtually disposable. Since there is no upward movement for staff attorneys, advancement opportunities must be found elsewhere.

Managing attorneys come to the franchise firms seeking a balance between a competitive market for clients and professional autonomy. What they find, however, is that in exchange for a steady flow of clients, prepackaged production systems and managerial authority severely constrain their professional independence. It is not having supervisors that alienates most managing attorneys. Rather, it is the experience of constantly having to fight for and protect branch office autonomy and profits from management's "greed" or irrationality that creates most of the disaffection among managing attorneys.

Each firm's partnership program seeks to counter the alienation experienced by managing attorneys by offering more local autonomy. But in each case there has been a price for greater local autonomy: the centralization of production outside of branch offices at Arthur & Nelson; and the shifting of financial risk for the operation of the law firm to local partners at Beck & Daniels. Next we look at another response to worker alienation—support of unions among branch office lawyers.

NOTES

1. Beck & Daniels requires that even experienced attorneys work initially as staff attorneys before moving into branch office management positions (see Chapter 2).

2. Regional and national managers at Beck & Daniels and Arthur & Nelson confirm the high rate of staff attorney turnover but argue that it does not pose problems for the firms. They suggest that the real threat to branch office operations is keeping qualified managing attorneys on the job.

3. It is interesting to note that female managing attorneys in highly profitable offices are more likely to share their earnings with office staff, while males in similar positions tend to offer time off.

4. The issue of how staff attorneys interpret their position in the franchise environment will be explored in more detail in Chapter 6.

5. Special units are discussed in Chapter 2 and below.

6. The term "black box" is used by managing attorneys to describe the way Beck & Daniels charges them for branch office costs. Rather than itemizing rent, computer and labor costs, the firm uses a standardized fee structure that is based on the number of attorneys in each local office. Managing attorneys never know exactly how office expenses are determined by management.

How many
g?

6

Alienation and Unions

During the 1980s, as women entered law in growing numbers, Arthur & Nelson and Beck & Daniels aggressively sought out female employees.[1] Firm management attempted both to exploit low-cost female labor and to capitalize on the view held by many clients that women appear to be more caring. To entice new female law school graduates to accept the modest income and status offered by these firms, interviewers discussed the "mission" of "helping clients overcome personal problems." In addition, interviewers for both firms promised "family friendly" work environments with 9:00 A.M. to 5:00 P.M. hours and opportunities for maternity leave. At Arthur & Nelson, employer-provided health insurance was also discussed as a future possibility.

Upon accepting employment, what the women encountered was quite different from the promises. Arthur & Nelson policy includes keeping branch offices open until 7:00 P.M. at least two evenings per week. Managing attorneys are strongly encouraged to open on Saturdays. At Beck & Daniels, two late evenings and Saturday hours are required of all employees on a rotating basis. The promises of health insurance and maternity leave never materialized.

Arthur & Nelson eventually threatened to demote managing attorneys who insisted on maternity leave to staff attorneys, because they would not be fulfilling their "professional duties" to clients.

The new women attorneys also found that they were limited in the amount of time they could spend working with clients. The franchise-style production systems were developed to lead clients through a standardized process, which Beck & Daniels advertised as "holding your hand from beginning to end." Accepting clients with complex divorce, child custody or other problems was discouraged as being beyond the scope of the production system and too time-consuming to be given adequate attention.

The women who refused to work evening hours or Saturdays (because they had been promised they would not have to) or who accepted cases more complex than the norm found themselves losing out on bonuses and recognition from management. Their offices simply were not generating as much revenue as offices operated by male managing attorneys. Among managing attorneys, the women were labeled as "too family oriented and not entrepreneurial enough," as an Arthur & Nelson managing attorney partner put it.

Alienated by broken promises (not to mention the limiting nature of the production process) and concerns that women and their interests were being subjugated to male attorneys and the profit motive, female attorneys at both firms attempted to organize unions.[2] At Arthur & Nelson the debate about unions was apparently firm-wide and created much conflict among managing attorneys. Beyond the major issue of whether or not to seek collective bargaining protections, attorneys disagreed on including or excluding secretaries in a union. In the end, however, the founding partners vetoed any attempts at collective bargaining and women quickly disappeared from the firm.

The unionization attempt did make a difference for the lawyers who remained with the firm. As a result, managing attorney compensation changed from salary to a percentage of office profits to encourage entrepreneurialism. In addition, the managing attorney partner position was created to reward successful employees who remained loyal to the firm.

The union drive at Beck & Daniels was limited to branch offices in one state. Beck & Daniels' response was to permanently close all offices in that state. Although Beck & Daniels remained highly centralized until the recent reorganization, the unionization attempt was symptomatic of the problems that finally resulted in the selling of branch offices to managing attorneys.

It appears that gender discrimination has played an important role in accentuating dissatisfaction among women lawyers at franchise law firms. However, there are also parallels to the analysis of alienation presented in the previous chapter. The women who led the collective bargaining campaigns were promised career paths that the firms could not or would not provide. There was no involvement of attorneys in these policy decisions; and the women who demanded the opportunities initially promised to them found themselves stigmatized and devalued by their peers. Given such a work environment, perhaps it is not surprising that almost 50 percent of the lawyers I interviewed view unions and collective bargaining positively.[3]

LAWYERS AND UNIONS

Although union organizing activity among professional workers increased through the 1970s and 1980s (Aronson 1985), among lawyers in the private bar, unionization efforts have traditionally been ineffectual.[4] Explanations for this reluctance to organize into collective bargaining units include the generous compensation and benefits enjoyed by many attorneys at law firms, the large number of private attorneys who are involved in solo practice or small partnership arrangements and the conflict between professional values and traditional union objectives (Rabban 1991, p. 97; Stavitsky 1980, p. 55). Wallace (1995) argues that law firms engender corporatist qualities that encourage job satisfaction and organizational commitment. The most important corporatist characteristics identified by Wallace include co-worker support, internal promotions, autonomy and participation in decision making.[5] Although Wallace does not consider the issue of unions, her findings appear applicable to the question of why lawyers have not shown much interest in developing collective bargaining arrangements.

The literature on professionalism and bureaucracy has traditionally assumed that professional and bureaucratic goals are in opposition to each other rather than complementary (Ben-David

1958; Blau and Scott 1962; Freidson 1994; March and Simon 1958; Oppenheimer 1973; Scott 1966). More recent research on lawyers has concluded that professionalism and bureaucracy may co-exist (Nelson 1988; Spangler 1986; also see Hall 1968; Montagna 1968). Wallace (1995) extends this debate by arguing: (1) Professionalism and corporatism are similar in work and organizational goals; (2) professional bureaucracies are imbued with corporatist qualities.

Wallace adapts Lincoln and Kalleberg's (1990, 1985) corporatist model of workplace control for manufacturing firms to law firms: "If the workplace is part of the professional community, provides professional career opportunities, allows for professional autonomy, and has values that are consistent with those of the profession, then it may alleviate the potential for professional-bureaucratic conflict" (1995, p. 812). Corporatist structures use normative, social and symbolic incentives to motivate workers.

In contrast to the corporatist qualities of traditional law firms, franchise law firms explicitly attempt to limit and control lawyer autonomy, provide few opportunities for collegial interactions among lawyers, offer virtually no opportunities for promotions and rarely include lawyers in firm-wide decision making. Just as positive relationships with these characteristics are related to job satisfaction for lawyers, negative relationships appear to be related to job dissatisfaction and pro-union sentiments among attorneys. In addition, gender discrimination appears to increase levels of alienation and willingness to seek union protection among lawyers. However, while the franchise organizational structure does not create "positive interdependence," it does provide incentives for some attorneys to view themselves as self-employed and to oppose collective bargaining.

LAW FIRM STRUCTURE AND UNION ATTITUDES

At first glance, a lawyer's structural position in Beck & Daniels or Arthur & Nelson appears to be a good predictor of attitudes toward unions.[6] Branch office managing attorneys tend to oppose collective bargaining while staff attorneys tend to support it. Sixty-six percent of managing attorneys oppose unionization, while 63 percent of staff attorneys support collective bargaining.

From an organizational standpoint, it only seems logical that managers might oppose unions and staff workers support unions. Managing attorneys have more (though still limited) decision-making power and responsibilities. In addition, the routinized production system to which all attorneys are subject at franchise law firms may explain why 34 percent of managing attorneys believe a union would be in their best interest. But if franchise law firms present such an oppressive work environment, why do one-third of the staff attorneys view unions negatively?

By examining the views expressed by managing attorneys and staff attorneys within each firm we can begin to answer this question. At Beck & Daniels, 80 percent of managing attorneys and 50 percent of staff attorneys *oppose* collective bargaining as a method of expressing or supporting their interests at the workplace. Yet at Arthur & Nelson, 82 percent of staff attorneys and 47 percent of managing attorneys *support* unionization of their workplace.

Although both firms have developed similar production and sales techniques, each firm also has developed different organizational structures. As previously discussed, Arthur & Nelson's partnership track is largely a job title change, not an ownership program. Arthur & Nelson branch office managing attorneys do not buy into the firm or have an equity stake in the firm as local partners do at Beck & Daniels. All Arthur & Nelson branch offices are owned by the firm's three founding partners. Among staff attorneys and some managing attorneys the knowledge that the founding partners ultimately make decisions concerning broad policy issues provides a common focus for frustration and anger about their conditions of work. This appears to be true even though at the branch office level successful managing attorneys have basic decision-making authority over issues such as hiring and firing (though they cannot readily choose to abandon the firm's production procedures). Thus pro-union Arthur & Nelson staff attorneys such as Greg and Rick (respectively) focus as much on firm management as on local office management:

I think [unions are] the wave of the future. . . . I think there's a need for it in a way, because it's just too arbitrary now. There is no job security, . . . the word could come down and you could be gone any day and that's no way to carry on. I think you didn't need it when there was more of a personal atmosphere among your employees, but now it's like, "let's make the bucks." So I could see it happening, sure, I think they probably need it.

I would say, yes, a union would help, but the whole point of getting a union in here would be completely absurd.

Because?

Oh, it would just never happen. They just wouldn't allow it. They would find a reason to terminate you before there was any kind of union that was able to happen. It reminds me of the whole history of the labor union. Like the garment industry, when one ethnic group would come in, like the Hungarians, and as soon as the Hungarian textile workers would want to unionize then they would fire them all. And then they would hire Czech workers. . . . They would just eliminate any kind of troublemaker.

They who?

Who? The owners. For us that would be the main office.

Arthur & Nelson staff attorneys believe that both they and managing attorneys are subject to the same, often arbitrary, authority of the founding partners and their management team. The presence of district managers who perform periodic file audits and the regular financial or "numbers" audits of the chief financial officer help to remind staff attorneys of the power held by those above the branch office level. That managing attorneys approach their relationship with management as inherently conflictual undoubtedly seems to enhance the staff attorney view of powerlessness. Brian (a staff attorney) provides an excellent example:

Would [a union] be in the workers' interests? Certainly. Would management tolerate it? No. Management is arbitrary, capricious. The CFO (Chief Financial Officer) is fond of coming down and saying [to the managing attorney], "Well look, your numbers weren't very good, somebody has to go—pick somebody." The power is localized in the hands of very, very few.

The almost 50 percent of Arthur & Nelson managing attorneys who view unionization or collective bargaining positively do not view the firm's management as "arbitrary [and] capricious," as is the case with many staff attorneys. Rather, managing attorneys see unions as providing the kind of collective voice that might help them to solve disputes with the main office more fairly and efficiently. Glenna would support a union or any other association of attorneys that might provide some leverage with management.

Well, lawyers have, as indeed many professionals have, they have absolutely no protection. And of course a union protects [against] things like having management take advantage of you. So in that sense, I suppose some organization would be good, to bargain more at arms length. Like just recently, there was a charge [to local offices] that was taken off that people were fighting about five years ago. That's not good. [It] shouldn't have taken that long.

Attorneys in less profitable offices, such as Gerald, see collective bargaining as perhaps the only way to force management to respect professional and branch office autonomy.

From the standpoint of what you just asked two minutes ago about staffing, technology, budget . . . could a union be useful? Yes, I don't have any real question about that. . . . The reality is that in this district most offices generally are not profitable, with one real exception. And under those circumstances perhaps some collective bargaining would be helpful.

Thus at Arthur & Nelson, pro-union staff attorneys and managing attorneys view collective bargaining as a tool which might allow those with less power in the firm to have a louder and stronger voice. Structurally, staff attorneys are in a position of having virtually no voice in the firm. Managing attorneys, on the other hand, view their voices as varying according to the profitability of their offices. Those with marginal or unprofitable offices often blame firm management for not giving them the autonomy to make the office more viable.

Indeed, the firm's method of rewarding managing attorneys who remain with the firm for at least five years and maintain highly profitable offices is to promote them to partner status. While managing attorney partners do not receive an equity stake in the firm, they are given greater freedom in operating their local offices. Managing attorney partners are not audited by district managers and have annual financial audits rather than quarterly audits. Interestingly, managing attorney partners and very profitable managing attorneys not only oppose unions but also do not express an interest in broad policy issues of the firm. For example, Phil, who believes "in our profession there should be no reason for unions," also has few concerns about policy input:

I feel that the three senior partners are capable of handling that and my input should be slight. But that's really what I feel they're earning their money on. . . . I just don't want to try to run everything. [They] are in a position where they know basically, and personally, the resources, they know what the capacities are, they know what their financial obligations are, which we don't. . . . If I'm not entirely aware of the financial ramifications, the liabilities and the assets, how can I give advice? And as far as the administration, you know I have some ideas, but this is what they're getting paid for. Let them perform, that's their end.

Managing attorney partners and very profitable managing attorneys believe that unions and the collective voice they offer are unnecessary as long as management provides the conditions and the tools for generating high revenues. Thus at Arthur & Nelson, anti-union lawyers view their position as relatively free of management interference, though they seek little or no voice in firm-wide policy agendas. Pro-union lawyers view their position as being subject to managerial control and therefore seek a medium that might provide them with a voice in firm-wide policy that would make them less subject to managerial control.

At Beck & Daniels the same issues are played out in a different organizational environment. Beck & Daniels has changed from a corporation style of organization and management that was more centralized than Arthur & Nelson to an actual franchise.[7] This arrangement encourages local partners to view themselves as self-employed. As firm owners, many local partners (and managing attorneys who anticipate being offered the chance to buy into the firm) oppose unions as antithetical to their interests. Matt notes how becoming an equity owner has changed his opinion about the need for unions.

If you would have asked me [about unions] after I had been working here a couple of years I would have said "definitely," because the staff was not listened to very much. . . . At this point I no longer think we need a union anymore. There was a time when I thought we did, but I don't think we do now.

Why not?

The employees I think as a whole feel much more positively about management than they did before.

Eric views unions as having the potential to organize his staff against his interests:

[A union] really wouldn't be helpful to me because I get everything I want within reason. . . . I don't think a union, which is designed to ensure worker's rights and fair working conditions, is really going to help me because we have a very informal arrangement around here. . . . I wouldn't think that my employees here, the staff I work with, would have any need for that here.

Like the managing attorney partners of Arthur & Nelson, Beck & Daniels' local partners have little interest in broad policy issues. Like Eric, most local partners simply wish to be left alone to operate their branch offices.

Beyond the four walls of my office I don't really care how the firm functions. It is not my problem. As long as I am left to my own devices in my office—I'm left to run my office the way I want it run within the framework of the manual that is set up by Beck & Daniels—I don't aspire to [input] and basically couldn't care less.

The equity ownership of Beck & Daniels offices and the lack of supervision of managing attorney partners at Arthur & Nelson lead these lawyers to focus on generating revenue at their local offices above all else.[8] In most cases they view their positions as being similar to that of self-employed attorneys rather than as employees of large law firms. As one managing attorney partner put it, "in a position such as mine, one is basically on his own." Attorneys who believe they have an independent interest in the operation of their branch offices tend to define themselves as management and oppose collective bargaining.

It is more difficult to explain the anti-union views of staff attorneys at Beck & Daniels. Most who expressed this view refused to explain their reasoning. Like Paul, those who offered an explanation generally referred to law as a profession rather than focusing on their actual work conditions.

I think [unions] are very good for organizing people, I just don't think they are necessary in law. I would hate to have that happen to lawyers, banding together as a union. I think it would confuse the real purpose of being a lawyer.

Yet these staff attorneys do not appear to be different from those who express support for unions at Beck & Daniels or staff attorneys at Arthur & Nelson. For example, Paul, the staff attorney quoted above expresses the same frustrations about his lack of autonomy and decision-making authority as other staff attorneys. When asked if input on broad policy issues is important to him, Paul responds that it doesn't matter because,

number one, I don't have any control. I don't know if they necessarily have a policy. It's more whatever the regional manager wants. I really don't know what policy they have with regard to staff and budgeting.

Another anti-union Beck & Daniels staff attorney complains that he is not even included in the process of hiring new branch office staff:

Truthfully, I don't think it's my concern right now. If they ask me I'll be glad to give them input but that's not what happens. . . . I know one thing for sure, though. When I become a managing attorney, when I'm getting ready to hire people and things like that, I would definitely ask for input from the other people in my office. Whether they like this person and they have a good feeling about this person . . . because one of the key ingredients is that everybody gets along or at least tries to get along.

These quotes suggest the frustration of staff attorneys at not being included in firm-wide policy decisions nor branch office management. The staff attorneys who support unions at Beck & Daniels express similar frustrations as justification for collective bargaining. For example, Andy believes a union may be useful "because we really have no vehicle at the present time that I'm aware of. . . . There's no formal, you know, there's no formal procedures for giving suggestions or anything."

The best explanation for the split in views toward unions among staff attorneys may be the reorganization of Beck & Daniels. At the time of these interviews there was a great amount of uncertainty about what selling branch offices to managing attorneys would mean for staff attorneys. Before the reorganization, Beck & Daniels policy mandated at least two staff attorneys be employed by each local office. The rationale for this policy was to ensure that attorneys would always be available for walk-in clients. This policy was rescinded as part of the reorganization. Many new local partners express the desire to trim office overhead by eliminating unnecessary labor costs. Although mass layoffs have not happened, in such an atmosphere some staff attorneys may fear that expressing support for a union will negatively affect their prospects of retaining a position with the firm. Others may view unions as inappropriate in a franchise organization. In any case, no staff attorneys in offices that had been sold to local partners expressed support for a union. Only a few staff attorneys working at offices which were expected to be reorganized in the near future expressed support of unions. Virtually all who viewed collective bargaining positively were employed at offices in which the reorganization campaign had not yet been announced (at least not to staff attorneys). It appears that the franchise organization discourages both managing attorneys and staff attorneys from interpreting collective bargaining positively. However, while franchising appears to increase the managing attorney's sense of autonomy and job satisfaction, there is no evidence that it affects staff attorneys in the same positive way.

Franchise law firms present their employees with few of the corporatist qualities Wallace (1995) associates with autonomous, small professional bureaucracies. Clearly, the limits franchise law firms place on lawyer autonomy, participation in decision making, internal advancement and co-worker support lead to higher levels of alienation from work than is apparent in other law firm settings (see e.g., Nelson 1988; Spangler 1986). The high level of support for unions among Arthur & Nelson managing and staff attorneys is no doubt a result of the discontinuity between professional expectations and the reality of the work environment. Nonetheless, firm organization appears to mediate how limits placed on professionalism are interpreted. The views expressed by Beck & Daniels local partners and Arthur & Nelson managing attorney partners suggest that franchise (or quasi-franchise) organizations may control or reduce alienation by substituting the appearance of self-employment for professional values. In the franchise environment, isolation from firm-wide policy issues is interpreted positively because it supports the local partner's and managing attorney partner's ideology of being a solo practitioner. This is important because franchise law firms provide no other opportunities for career advancement and the proprietary production systems necessarily limit professional autonomy.

The limitations placed on attorney decision making, work interactions and career mobility by franchise law firms appears to frustrate and alienate many lawyers to the point where they believe collective bargaining would be beneficial. Lawyers employed by franchise law firms appear to want the protection of unions based on their perceptions of degradation at the workplace.

Nonetheless, attorneys employed by franchise law firms do not unanimously support unions. In place of corporatist methods of labor control the franchise organization substitutes a classical ideology of petite bourgeois ownership (see Mills 1951). Attorneys at both Arthur & Nelson and Beck & Daniels experience similar constraints to professionalism. Yet many staff attorneys and some managing attorneys support the concept of collective bargaining, while local partners and managing attorney partners do not. Furthermore, local partners and managing attorney partners do not express an interest in being included in firm-wide policy decisions. Inclusion would serve as a reminder that local partners and managing attorney partners are not truly "independent" practitioners but are subject to controlling and limiting production systems. Rather, it is the pro-union attorneys who seek a voice in policy decisions, largely because they cannot interpret their positions as being independent of firm management.

The franchise equity buy-in program also apparently quells desire for union activities among staff attorneys. Unfortunately, this is not accomplished by providing them with a sense of power and independence, but through isolation, fear and hopelessness. Franchising by Beck & Daniels has removed firm management as a focal point for complaints and anger about being exploited and treated as labor rather than being treated as colleagues.[9]

Finally, women were hired by both firms to exploit their low labor-market values and the perception of clients that female lawyers are more caring and trustworthy. But broken promises of family-oriented work environments and a resulting loss of compensation and status in each firm has led women to seek union protections. Although the union campaigns failed, they helped push both firms toward the franchise organizational structure. To this day, the more entrepreneurial franchise organization (as opposed to the traditional professional bureaucratic structure) is faulted with disadvantaging female lawyers at these firms. Only one of the female lawyers I interviewed was a managing attorney partner or local partner. Nonetheless, all of these attorneys except the one local partner strongly support collective bargaining to provide them with a voice in their respective firms.

It seems apparent that when lawyers are treated as labor to be exploited rather than as valued expert resources they become frustrated, alienated and, sometimes, angry, as do other workers who are not treated with dignity and respect. These are the conditions in which collective bargaining campaigns are often born. Yet the franchise structure potentially averts unionization attempts by offering an opportunity for branch office managers to interpret their positions as individual practitioners. Despite Carlin's (1994) proclamation that the individual practitioner's glory days ended 30 years ago, it is nonetheless a more positive ideological orientation than the alternative provided by franchise law firms. But franchise law firm branch offices are not independent practices. They are market-researched outlets for mass-marketed and mass-produced legal services. Only the ideology of the "self-made man" (Carlin 1994, p. 3) of solo practice lives on through local partners and managing attorney partners.

NOTES

1. This discussion is largely based upon anecdotal accounts by male managing attorneys (including local partners and managing attorney partners) and upper-level firm managers. At on time both firms employed about as many female as male lawyers. However, since the failed unionization attempts (to be described in this section), currently only about 10 percent of lawyers employed by each firm are female. Of the 55 lawyers I interviewed, only 6 are female.

2. Although reports vary in consistency, the union-organizing attempts

at Arthur & Nelson began in 1985. At Beck & Daniels organizing began in 1986.

3. Forty-seven percent of lawyers in my sample view collective bargaining positively, 53 percent oppose unions.

4. Despite a lack of interest by most lawyers in union representation and collective bargaining, the National Labor Relations Board (NLRB) asserted jurisdiction over private law firms in 1977. See Stavitsky (1980) for a discussion of the NLRB rulings on collective bargaining by lawyers.

5. Wallace's (1995) survey of law firm lawyers in Alberta, Canada found that the amount and distribution of financial rewards is not a significant determinant of job satisfaction and organizational commitment among lawyers.

6. Wallace (1995, p. 832, note 18) also finds evidence that structural position in law firms affects job satisfaction. (See also Poor 1994.)

7. Beck & Daniels does not plan to franchise all offices. Some may be kept by firm management for the training of new managing attorneys before they buy offices as local partners.

8. The incentive structure of franchises also encourages a focus on profits (see chapters 2 and 3).

9. This is similar to the experience of McDonald's kitchen workers. See Garson (1988).

7

Markets, Innovation and Prepackaged Law

Franchise law firms bring legal services into our mass consuming society. The commodity system is where consumers expect to satisfy most of their daily needs (Ewen 1976). That the goods and services available are increasingly prepackaged has not deterred their purchases. Franchises continue to enjoy incredible popularity and growth (see, e.g., Ritzer 1996; Cullen 1996). The success of franchise law firms at gaining clients and the adoption of their techniques by plaintiff's personal injury firms (Van Hoy 1996) suggest that legal services are not immune to the twentieth-century trend toward creating a mass society.

For most middle-income consumers the prepackaging of legal services offers many potential benefits. Advertising increases awareness that legal needs can be solved by procuring professional services. Standardization of services focuses consumers on price competition rather than quality and may even ensure that some basic level of quality is being maintained. Most importantly, however, prepackaged law offers consumers what they have come to expect: an atmosphere that is appealing, courteous and efficient. The branch office secretary's calm voice and friendly smile combine with the attorney's sales pitch to make purchasing legal services relatively pleasant. As long as clients do not have expectations of individualized expert service they are likely to be satisfied with their experiences (see Chapter 3). In part this satisfaction may be the outcome of not knowing what to expect. Most clients have not dealt with attorneys many times before. Franchise law firms have the advantage of being able to shape the expectations of their inexperienced clients; to define their legal problems as routine and easily solved. Recall the Beck & Daniels attorney who told me that I would make a poor client because I "would want to be too involved." Most clients are just the opposite: They are eager to be advised. Indeed, the view that professions monopolize markets for expert services correctly conceptualizes this process as professional dominance (Freidson 1994). Monopoly approaches focus on the historical process in which professions gain wealth and status by claiming exclusive rights to provide expert services (Abbott 1988; Abel 1989; Larson 1977; Starr 1982).

These approaches treat the professions as institutions (or systems) that have achieved social closure and are protected from competition. But the analysis of franchise law firms suggests that the issue professional markets should not be ignored (see Nelson 1988 for a similar approach to corporate law firms). As the barriers to entering the profession and seeking clients have fallen, labor markets and client markets have become more important. While professional dominance and monopoly theories help to explain the experiences of clients, they do little to help us understand the experiences of lawyers and secretaries at franchise law firms.

At the beginning of this study I suggested that franchise law firms (along with other "new providers" of legal services) may be displacing the lower-level practitioners identified in early studies of the legal profession (Carlin 1994). These practitioners acted mainly as service brokers rather than providing legal services themselves. Of the new providers of legal services, prepaid legal services plans may offer the most direct comparison to brokering. These plans help to connect lawyers in private practice with middle-income clients. Franchise law firms also seek to serve this new client base that traditionally has not sought legal services. But in doing so they exploit the buyer's market for attorneys by imposing technologies previously not applied to law. Because franchise law firms have a unique role in the legal profession, it is important to understand them in historical and market contexts.

INNOVATION VERSUS DEGRADATION

Personal legal services work has long been considered routine and less skilled than corporate legal services (Carlin 1994; Heinz and Laumann 1982; Reed 1921; see also Chapter 1). Franchise law firms have developed in the personal services market of the legal profession by building upon existing conditions. Although attorneys experience franchise law firms as degrading, this is not the result of de-skilling legal issues so much as the innovative re-organization of work practices. Clearly, computer technology plays a role in the efficiency and productivity of branch offices. However, boilerplate documents and form books existed long before franchise law firms (see, e.g., Carlin 1994, 1966). Indeed, we have seen that solo and small-firm practitioners also use computers whenever possible. Franchise law firms openly acknowledge the division in the legal profession between skilled and de-skilled work; between serving large organizations and serving individuals.

Franchise law firms became possible in the personal legal services market with the intersection of two events. As access to law school has become less exclusive the result has been the steady growth of competition among attorneys for jobs and clients. In addition, in 1977 the potential for creating mass markets of legal consumers through television advertising became tangible. Building upon the model of legal clinics, franchise law firms exploit both the market of untapped legal consumers and the cheap supply of legal labor.

What makes franchise law firms unique is the organization of legal and administrative work tasks. Prepackaged law is the mass marketing and mass production of routine legal services. This includes the application of new strategies for raising capital for expanding the networks of branch offices as well as the standardization of production. We have seen that the experiences of attorneys at franchise law firms are mixed at best. The vast majority of attorneys find practicing prepackaged law restrictive, repetitive and boring. The use of standardized production systems limits attorney autonomy to "mak[ing] a sale or just telling them [clients] we can't help them." Secretaries often appear to have more decision-making authority than do attorneys. This degrading aspect of prepackaged law stems from the highly rationalized and limited organization of work and career paths these innovations impose on branch offices. For example, staff attorneys find the limits placed on professional autonomy are exacerbated by limited potential for increased pay and promotion opportunities. Staff attorneys quickly learn that they are expendable laborers in a mass-production setting. It is not uncommon for staff attorneys to compare their experiences to workers in textile, steel or other mass-production industries before unions were formed.

In contrast to staff attorneys, it is secretaries who express the most satisfaction with their work experiences. Although secretaries also work long hours for relatively low pay, they are aware of the pivotal role they play in branch office operations. Secretaries interpret their position as being the "true" branch office managers. After all, secretaries take responsibility for dealing with the day-to-day needs of branch offices and management. To minimize their contact with management, managing attorneys place the burden of "finding answers to administrative problems" on their secretaries. At the same time, the organization of branch office duties by management gives secretaries primary responsibility for bookkeeping, bank deposits, supplies and repairs.

Secretaries also have important duties that relate to serving clients. They make the first contact with clients when they telephone or walk in the door. It is the secretary who managing attorneys credit most with keeping clients satisfied through a positive demeanor and frequent client contacts (by telephone). Attorneys acknowledge that secretaries create most of the legal documents. Staff attorneys find secretaries to be most helpful in orienting them to the franchise environment and helping to appropriately serve clients. It is no wonder that attorneys complain that they are too limited in their efforts to serve clients, while secretaries marvel at all the people they have helped at the end of each day.

Alienation versus Entrepreneurialism

Successful managing attorneys, local partners and managing attorney partners accept the consequences of prepackaged law because the franchise organization offers acceptable trade-offs in terms of potential income stability and ideological satisfaction. Branch office managers find that operating profitable offices results in less supervision from firm management. This in turn allows them to interpret their position as "basically the same" as solo practice. Arthur & Nelson and Beck & Daniels, with their partnership programs, have developed organizational and incentive strategies that encourage the branch office manager's "independent entrepreneur" orientation.

Branch office managers in less profitable offices and staff attorneys have a different set of experiences. Staff attorneys may accept the managing attorney ideal of operating a small business, but they learn to look for those opportunities outside of the franchise setting. Managing attorneys in less profitable offices find they are faced with expectations that they will act as entrepreneurs at the same time that they are losing any sense of autonomy. In these cases the entrepreneurial incentives of the franchise organization do not counteract experiences of alienation. Managing attorneys generally view firm management as competitors for limited resources. In branch offices with questionable profit margins, firm managers may make decisions without input from the managing attorneys. In these cases, managing attorneys tend to retain the ideal of operating a small business and claim that management is restraining their ability to improve profits.

In many marginal branch offices managing attorneys speak of returning to solo practice. However, these attorneys do not care to return to individual practice situations without some of the advantages of the franchise environment. Managing attorneys at both firms voice concern that the standardized production systems and limited menus of services have kept them from remaining competent in other practice areas. At Arthur & Nelson the concern is that local offices have become divorce specialists while special units handle other lucrative areas of law (particularly plaintiff's personal injury and personal bankruptcy). Beck & Daniels attorneys are limited to the seven general case types available on computer (and only in the formats available on computer).

Disgruntled managing attorneys at both firms quietly spoke of their efforts to "break the firm's security" on proprietary computer programs. The idea, they said, was to go out into solo practice with an advantage. Arthur & Nelson attorneys are most interested in the forms and letters for divorce, wills and residential real estate closings. Beck and Daniels managing attorneys told stories of attempting to copy or steal all of the integrated programs for their firm's menu of services. All of these attorneys had found that the programs were copy protected. Thus, a few attorneys had swapped hard drives, putting an unformatted drive of the same size and manufacture in place of the original. With the firms' hard drives and the programs they contain running in computers at their homes they hoped to learn how to change the letterhead and logo features. As one of these managing attorneys put it,

the idea is to run the same business I do here—there is nothing wrong with the forms we are using in the office—I just don't want to pay my profits to this firm. I can run a business better than they can. On the other hand, I don't want to have to make the investment in creating and debugging the computer programs. I'd have quite an advantage if I can do it this way. They already have everything integrated.

The entrepreneurial emphasis of the franchise organization only offers the incentives of profits and a sense of self-determination. When attorneys are not able to achieve high profit margins—which leads to less supervision of local offices—the entrepreneurial ideology becomes the basis of managing attorney alienation from the franchise work environment.

For many managing attorneys, managing attorney partners and local partners, the line separating acceptance of the limits of prepackaged law and perceptions of alienation is very thin. Branch offices succeed or fail on services that have small profit margins. Local economies and the decisions of firm management can (and do) affect the ability of branch offices to meet revenue and profit goals.

Organizational Change versus Demise

The line between alienation and acceptance is most often narrowed during times of great uncertainty. As Beck & Daniels and Arthur & Nelson have moved to capture new markets, increase productivity and find new ways of financing their law firms, their organizational structures have also changed. At both firms the recession of 1990–1992 hastened the development of reorganization plans. It was during this time that Arthur & Nelson finished centralizing production in special units and began to focus advertising on personal injury and bankruptcy (rather than divorce). At the same time, Beck & Daniels began to consolidate offices in preparation for the selling of profitable branch offices to managing attorneys. During the recession, along with many other law firms, Arthur & Nelson stopped growing; Beck & Daniels closed many offices as its policy of overstaffing now eliminated all profits (Brill 1991a, 1991b, 1989; Clarke 1991; Rutman 1991).

The legal press and other observers quickly declared the demise of franchise law firms during this period (see, e.g., Seron 1996, pp. 1–2). However, a more careful examination reveals that franchise law firms have not ceased to exist, but have evolved in response to challenges from the market they helped to define. As the innovations of franchise law firms have been disseminated, the level of competition has intensified. In response, Arthur & Nelson sought both new markets and more effective production techniques. Beck & Daniels moved to shift the financial burden of capitalizing the law firm to the managing attorneys.

Change, of course, implies a certain level of demise. Old methods and strategies are abandoned for new ones. Beck & Daniels branch offices are now largely employee-owned. Arthur & Nelson has transformed itself into what it calls the largest plaintiff's personal injury law firm in the United States. Nonetheless, the basic concepts on which these firms were founded remains unchanged. Routine legal services continue to be mass marketed and mass produced. Arthur & Nelson's plaintiff's personal injury practice is founded on negotiating small settlements with insurance companies. A team of secretaries is supervised by a few attorneys to bring in as many fees as possible while keeping overhead costs low. Beck & Daniels continues to impose its production system on locally owned offices through local partner contracts (see Chapter 2).

Franchise law firms, like many mass consumer industries, are subject to the cycles of boom and bust in the economy. Franchise law firms are among the high-growth, high-risk ventures that have created many job opportunities in recent years (Lorant 1996). However, the competitive market in which these firms were born forces them to constantly seek new products, increase levels of productivity and lower overhead costs. Stability cannot be maintained for long periods of time. Arthur & Nelson is an excellent example. After first emphasizing divorce, during the 1990 recession the firm first began to shift its focus to personal bankruptcy filings and then to plaintiff's personal injury as the economy rebounded. Firm managers successfully followed the changing needs or wants of middle-income legal consumers. In addition, bankruptcy and plaintiff's personal injury processing can be centralized much more easily than divorce services. Filing papers with the courts or negotiating with insurance companies requires less personal contact between lawyer/secretary and client than negotiating divorce settlements. Arthur & Nelson continues to move in two directions: separating the lawyer from the legal services the firm provides and dehumanizing the procurement of services by clients.

A leaner Beck & Daniels continues to emphasize its system of offering seven general types of services. In contrast to Arthur & Nelson, Beck & Daniels has been most innovative in developing new capital resources for the law firm and shifting responsibility for controlling overhead costs to local office managers. Rather than emphasizing one or two specific types of services, Beck & Daniels seeks to shift the financial burdens of their branch offices and their marketing needs to new members of the law firm. How long they can continue the current strategy of presenting themselves as a "neighborhood" law firm may depend on how long the economy continues to improve. To date, Beck & Daniels management has been more willing to find new investors than reconsider the firm's marketing and production strategies.

PROFESSIONAL STATUS AND CAPITALISM

Wallace (1995, p. 830) suggests that the distinction between professional workers and other workers may be blurring. Corporatist control methods may bring professional values to non-professional employees such as auto assembly workers. This study offers an interesting twist on that conclusion. Some professional workers are becoming subject to methods of control that are rigid, and that exclude employees from decisions and treat professional workers as disposable. The gap between professional and non-professional workers is narrowing because of movement in two directions.

Some non-professional workers are becoming subject to corporatist or professional control methods at the same time that some professional employees are encountering work settings which do not support corporatist values. We have seen that the most highly exploited attorneys have even developed a pro-union ideology.

The nature of capitalist production is to constantly revolutionize technology and organization to obtain greater productivity and profits. Depending on the requirements to carry out tasks, this can mean protecting worker autonomy or reducing it. It is unreasonable to assume that a profession's status in society permanently shelters its practitioners from competing for profits (if it ever did). The constant attacks on "ambulance chasers" throughout the twentieth century (see, e.g., Auerbach 1976) suggests that personal services lawyers have constantly struggled to survive. When advertising and fees were controlled by bar associations, personal services lawyers were forced to compete as small firms and solo practitioners because mass markets of legal consumers could not be reached. But this does not mean that there was no competition among service providers.

Will Solo and Small-Firm Practices Survive?

A number of observers have noted a trend toward the decline of solo practice in the professions (Derber 1982). In the legal profession solo practice has also declined, though it continues to comprise the largest group of attorneys in private practice (Abel 1989; Curran and Carson 1991). This has been interpreted as a sign that professional workers may be more subject to de-skilling than in the past as they become employees of large, bureaucratic firms. This study may lend some support to that conclusion. However, in the legal profession there has always been a segment of practitioners who have not exercised a high level of skill *and they have traditionally been solo and small-firm practitioners*. It is not simply the size of firms that determines levels of autonomy or degradation. A number of studies have shown that other large, bureaucratic professional firms do not significantly limit their employees' autonomy (Freidson 1986; Nelson 1988; Spangler 1986). Franchise law firms reorganize low-skill legal tasks for mass-production purposes. This suggests that markets may be more important determinants of degradation or autonomy at work than firm size or bureaucracy alone. Franchise law firms can only mass produce the most basic of legal services. They leave the somewhat more sophisticated (though still highly routine) work to those remaining outside of their firms. In addition, the rush of new attorneys into the profession and the high turnover of attorneys from the franchise firms suggests that solo and small-firm practice will continue to dominate the personal services market.

The larger problem is that there is no relief in sight for any personal services lawyers. Personal legal services continues to be a difficult area of law to practice in. Among the attorneys I have spoken with—whether in solo, small-firm or franchise law firm practices—there are very high levels of dissatisfaction. Of those with children, only a few say that they do or will encourage them to become lawyers in the future.

Appendix:
Data and Methods

The data described and analyzed in this book were collected from October of 1990 through November of 1991, though I have contacted some of the study participants over the intervening years to keep abreast of changes as I prepared this volume. The two firms studied here (Arthur & Nelson and Beck & Daniels are pseudonyms) were chosen because of their leadership in developing the franchise law firm market for services. Both firms are national in scope and each firm employed 300–400 attorneys during the period of the study.

To gain access I approached the owners of each firm about the possibility of participating in the study. I proposed in-office observation and interviewing because little was known about the work routines, organization and relationships of lawyers and office staff at these new legal services firms. Negotiations with management of each firm ensued over a six-month period. Eventually, I gained permission to observe in two Arthur & Nelson offices and one Beck & Daniels office. In addition, I conducted numerous informal follow-up visits with the Beck & Daniels office staff, which also led to informal visits at three other Beck & Daniels branch offices.

(Beck & Daniels management was aware of these visits and did not object.) Both firms also agreed to provide lists of office personnel in a broader array of offices for in-depth interviews.

OFFICE OBSERVATIONS

While at each office, I moved about freely, observing interactions and watching work being prepared. I openly asked questions of attorneys and staff. I also observed consultations between lawyers and clients. I was on hand when the first person arrived to open each office and left with the last person to go home at night.

I kept extensive field notes of all office visits and contacts with the study population. Sometimes I would sit at empty desks to write field notes during the day because managing attorneys wanted me to look like a part of the office. That is, managing attorneys wanted clients to see office personnel who were busy, not standing around watching others work. Because I dressed similarly to the attorneys, some managing attorneys were concerned that clients might be angered if I appeared unproductive.

Which consultations I observed were largely determined by the attorneys I worked with and the clients' wishes. The attorneys decided which consultations were appropriate for observation, introduced me to the clients and asked their permission. This was a subjective process. Some attorneys would not let me observe divorce consultations because the client might become "emotional" and feel uncomfortable with my presence in the office. Other attorneys asked virtually all clients if "the sociologist" might observe the consultation. When asked, clients usually agreed to let me watch the consultation. My field notes recall only three instances where the clients declined to have me present during consultations.

INTERVIEWS

Subsequent to the office visits I asked both firms for permission to interview a larger sample of attorneys, staff and managers using a semi-structured interview schedule. Arthur & Nelson cooperated by providing a list of all personnel in a sixteen-office geographic area. Beck & Daniels was somewhat less cooperative, allowing me to interview only a small, hand-picked group of 25 lawyers and managers who, by their own admission, represent the most successful members of the firm. (Beck & Daniels refused my request to interview secretaries.)

To some extent the Beck & Daniels interview sample bias is balanced by the office visits. The offices I observed in, by all accounts, were struggling to maintain profitability. I attempted to broaden the interview samples of both Beck & Daniels and Arthur & Nelson with snowball sampling techniques. Snowball sampling led to my interviewing both former employees and employees not originally offered by management of the two firms.[1] By asking respondents to recommend other people associated with the firm to interview, I increased the sample of Beck & Daniels personnel to 39 lawyers and managers (most managers are also lawyers) and two secretaries. My sample of Arthur & Nelson respondents includes 15 secretaries and 28 attorneys and managers. A total of 85 franchise law firm respondents were interviewed for this study.

INDIVIDUAL AND SMALL-FIRM PRACTITIONER INTERVIEWS

To gain a better understanding of the market for personal legal services I also interviewed a random sample of 35 solo-practicing and small-firm attorneys in the Chicago metropolitan area. A sample size of 30—ten attorneys from each of three broad geographic areas—was originally targeted to gain a broad overview of law practices in Chicago. The three areas include downtown Chicago (the Loop), Chicago outside of the Loop and the suburbs. Post office maps and zip codes were used to determine the boundaries of each area. Attorneys were selected from the 1991 edition of *Sullivan's Law Directory*. The publisher of *Sullivan's Law Directory* claims that 98 percent of all attorneys residing in Illinois are listed in the directory. A random sample was selected from the index listing all attorneys in the six-county Chicago metropolitan area. After consecutively numbering all of the attorneys listed in the Chicago area index (over 49,000), 150 numbers were selected using a random numbers table.

Attorneys listed as members of firms with more than ten lawyers were eliminated from the list. Attorneys listed as retired, deceased or over 70 years of age were also eliminated. The 55 remaining attorneys were categorized as follows: 22 had addresses in the Loop, 18 had addresses outside of the Loop in Chicago and 15 had suburban addresses. Letters describing the study and requesting interviews were sent to all 55 attorneys. Ten Loop attorneys, thirteen Chicago attorneys and twelve suburban attorneys were eventually interviewed using Jerome Carlin's (1994) semi-structured interview schedule from his classic study of solo practitioners in Chicago, *Lawyers on Their Own*. All interviews were tape-recorded and transcribed with the permission of the respondents.[2]

NOTES

1. Firm managers were aware of my sample design and did not object to the use of snowball sampling techniques. However, many Beck & Daniels upper-level managers expressed surprise when employees consented to interviews without seeking prior approval.

2. For a more detailed discussion of my research methods and interview schedules, see Van Hoy 1993.

References

Abbott, A. 1988. *The System of Professions*. Chicago: University of Chicago Press.

Abel, R. L. 1989. *American Lawyers*. New York: Oxford University Press.

———. 1988a. "United States: The Contradictions of Professionalism." In *Lawyers in Society, Vol. 1: The Common Law World*, edited by R. Abel and P. S. C. Lewis. Berkeley: University of California Press.

———. 1988b. "England and Wales: A Comparison of the Professional Projects of Barristers and Solicitors." In *Lawyers in Society, Vol. 1: The Common Law World*, edited by R. Abel and P. S. C. Lewis. Berkeley: University of California Press.

———. 1981. "Toward a Political Economy of Lawyers." *Wisconsin Law Review* 5: 1117–1187.

American Bar Association. 1990. *Report on the Survey of Legal Clinics and Advertising Law Firms*. Chicago: American Bar Association.

———. 1982. *Legal Clinics: Merely Advertising Law Firms?* Chicago: American Bar Association.

Aronson, R. L. 1985. "Unionism Among Professional Employees in the Private Sector." *Industrial and Labor Relations Review* 38: 352–364.

Auerbach, J. S. 1976. *Unequal Justice: Lawyers and Social Change in Modern America*. New York: Oxford University Press.

Bates & O'Steen v. Arizona State Bar, 433 U.S. 350 (1977).

Ben-David, J. 1958. "The Professional Role of the Physician in Bureaucratic Medicine." *Human Relations* 11: 255–274.

Blau, P. M. and W. R. Scott. 1962. *Formal Organizations: A Comparative Approach.* Chicago: University of Chicago Press.

Brill, S. 1991a. "Headnotes." *American Lawyer* (June): 3, 56.

———. 1991b. "Short-Term Pain, Long-Term Gain." *American Lawyer* (January): 5–6, 55–59.

———. 1989. "The Law Business in the Year 2000." *American Lawyer* (June): 10.

Cain, M. 1983. "The General Practice Lawyer and the Client: Towards a Radical Conception." In *The Sociology of the Professions*, edited by R. Dingwall and P. Lewis. New York: St. Martin's Press.

Carlin, J. 1994. *Lawyers on Their Own: A Study of Individual Practitioners in Chicago* (second edition). San Francisco: Austin and Winfield.

———. 1966. *Lawyer's Ethics: A Survey of the New York City Bar.* New York: Russell Sage Foundation.

Carr-Saunders, A. M. and P. A. Wilson. 1933. *The Professions.* Oxford: Oxford University Press.

Clarke, C. V. 1991. "Shattered Dreams." *American Lawyer* (June): 58–63.

Cullen, K. 1996. "U.S. Cities Surrender Personalities." *Journal and Courier* (Lafayette, IN) (September 9): A1–A2.

Curran, B. A. 1977. *The Legal Needs of the Public.* Chicago: American Bar Foundation.

Curran, B. A. and C. N. Carson. 1991. *Supplement to the Lawyer Statistical Report: The U.S. Legal Profession in 1988.* Chicago: American Bar Foundation.

Derber, C. 1982. *Professionals at Work: Mental Labor in Advanced Capitalism.* Boston: G. K. Hall.

Ewen, S. 1976. *Captains of Consciousness.* New York: McGraw-Hill.

Freidson, E. 1994. *Professionalism Reborn.* Chicago: University of Chicago Press.

———. 1986. *Professional Powers.* Chicago: University of Chicago Press.

———. 1970. *Profession of Medicine: A Study in the Sociology of Applied Knowledge.* New York: Dodd Mead.

Galanter, M. 1974. "Why the 'Haves' Come Out Ahead: Speculations on the Limits of Legal Change." *Law and Society Review* 9: 96–160.

Galanter, M. and T. Palay. 1992. *Tournament of Lawyers: The Growth and Transformation of the Big Law Firm.* Chicago: University of Chicago Press.

Garson, B. 1988. *The Electronic Sweatshop*. New York: Penguin Books.

Hall, R. H. 1968. "Professionalization and Bureaucratization." *American Sociological Review* 33: 92–104.

Haug, M. R. 1977. "Computer Technology and the Obsolescence of the Concept of Profession." In *Work and Technology*, edited by M. R. Haug and J. Dofny. Beverly Hills, CA: Sage.

———. 1975. "The Deprofessionalization of Everyone?" *Sociological Focus* 8: 197-213.

———. 1973. "Deprofessionalization: An Alternative Hypothesis for the Future." *Sociological Review Monongraph* 20: 195–212.

Heinz, J. P. and E. O. Laumann. 1982. *Chicago Lawyers: The Social Structure of the Bar*. New York and Chicago: Russell Sage Foundation & American Bar Foundation.

Jacob, H. 1990. "The Contours of Divorce Lawyering." Working paper on file at the Center for Urban Affairs and Policy Research, Northwestern University, Evanston, IL.

Katz, J. 1982. *Poor People's Lawyers in Transition*. New Brunswick, NJ: Rutgers University Press.

Ladinsky, J. 1976. "The Traffic in Legal Services: Lawyer Seeking Behavior and the Channeling of Clients." *Law and Society Review* 11: 207–223.

Landon, D. D. 1990. *Country Lawyers: The Impact of Context on Professional Practice*. New York: Praeger.

Larson, M. S. 1977. *The Rise of Professionalism*. Berkeley: University of California Press.

Leidner, R. 1993. *Fast Food, Fast Talk: Service Work and the Routinization of Everyday Life*. Berkeley: University of California Press.

Lincoln, J. R. and A. L. Kalleberg. 1990. *Control and Commitment: A Study of Work Organization and Work Attitudes in the United States and Japan*. Cambridge, MA: Cambridge University Press.

———. 1985. "Work Organization and Workforce Commitment: A Study of Plants and Employees in the US and Japan." *American Sociological Review* 50: 738–760.

Lorant, R. 1996. "Study: 3 Percent of Firms Provide 80 Percent of U.S. Job Growth." *Journal and Courier* (Lafayette, IN) (October 14): A9.

Macaulay, S. 1979. "Lawyers and Consumer Protection Laws." *Law and Society Review* 14: 115–171.

March, J. G. and H. A. Simon. 1958. *Organizations*. New York: John Wiley and Sons.

McIntyre, L. J. 1987. *The Public Defender: The Practice of Law in the Shadows of Repute*. Chicago: University of Chicago Press.

Mills, C. W. 1951. *White Collar: The American Middle Classes.* New York: Oxford University Press.

Montagna, P.D. 1968. "Professionalization and Bureaucratization in Large Professional Organizations." *American Journal of Sociology* 74: 138–145.

Nelson, R. L. 1988. *Partners with Power: The Social Transformation of the Large Law Firm.* Berkeley: University of California Press.

Nelson, R. L. and D. Trubek. 1992. "Arenas of Professionalism: The Professional Ideologies of Lawyers in Collective and Workplace Contexts." In *Lawyers' Ideals and Lawyers' Practices*, edited by R. Nelson, R. Solomon and D. Trubek. Ithaca, NY: Cornell University Press.

O'Gorman, H. 1963. *Lawyers and Matrimonial Cases.* New York: The Free Press.

Oppenheimer, M. 1973. "The Proletarianization of the Professional." *Sociological Review Monograph* 20: 4.

Parsons, T. 1954. "The Professions and Social Structure." In *Essays in Sociological Theory*, edited by T. Parsons. New York: The Free Press.

Pashigian, B. P. 1978. "The Number and Earnings of Lawyers: Some Recent Findings." *American Bar Foundation Research Journal* (Winter 1978): 51–82.

Poor, D. C. 1994. "Organizational Culture and Professional Selves: The Impact of Large Law Firm Practice Upon Young Lawyers." Ph.D. dissertation, City University of New York.

Rabban, D. M. 1991. "Is Unionization Compatible with Professionalism?" *Industrial and Labor Relations Review* 45: 97–112.

Reed, A. Z. 1921. *Training for the Public Profession of the Law.* New York: Carnegie Foundation for the Advancement of Teaching.

Reidinger, S. 1987. "More Lawyers Now Advertise Their Practice." *American Bar Association Journal* 73: 25.

Ritzer, G. 1996. *The McDonaldization of Society* (revised edition). Thousand Oaks, CA: Pine Forge Press.

Rosenthal, D. 1974. *Lawyers and Clients: Who's in Charge?* New York: Russell Sage Foundation.

Rutman, K. 1991. "The Boom Abates." *National Law Journal* (September): S2–S4.

Sander, R. H. and D. Williams. 1989. "Why Are There So Many Lawyers? Perspectives on a Turbulent Market." *Law and Social Inquiry* 14: 431–479.

Sarat, A. and W. L. F. Felstiner. 1995. *Divorce Lawyers and Their Clients:*

Power and Meaning in the Legal Process. New York: Oxford University Press.

———. 1986. "Law and Strategy in the Divorce Lawyer's Office." *Law and Society Review* 20: 93–134.

Scott, R. W. 1966. "Professionals in Bureaucracies—Areas of Conflict." In *Professionalization*, edited by H. M. Vollmer and D. L. Mills. New York: Prentice-Hall.

Seron, C. 1996. *The Business of Practicing Law: The Work Lives of Solo and Small-Firm Attorneys.* Philadelphia: Temple University Press.

———. 1993. "New Strategies for Getting Clients: Urban and Suburban Lawyers' Views." *Law and Society Review* 27: 399–419.

Smigel, E. 1969. *The Wall Street Lawyer: Professional Organizational Man?* (second edition). Bloomington: Indiana University Press.

Solomon, R. L. 1992. "Five Crises or One: The Concept of Legal Professionalism, 1925–1960." In *Lawyers' Ideals and Lawyers' Practices*, edited by R. Nelson, R. Solomon and D. Trubek. Ithaca, NY: Cornell University Press.

Spangler, E. 1986. *Lawyers for Hire.* New Haven, CT: Yale University Press.

Starr, P. 1982. *The Social Transformation of American Medicine.* New York: Basic Books.

Stavitsky, B. J. 1980. "Lawyer Unionization in Quasi-Governmental Public and Private Sectors." *California Western Law Review* 17: 55–74.

Sullivan's Law Directory. 1991. (114th edition). Barrington, IL: Law Bulletin Publishing Co.

Terkel, S. 1972. *Working: People Talk About What They Do All Day and How They Feel About What They Do.* New York: Avon Books.

Van Hoy, J. 1996. "Plaintiff's Personal Injury Attorneys in Indiana: Overzealous Advocates or Principle Protectors of the Individual?" Paper presented at the Law and Society Association Annual Meetings, July 10–13, Glasgow, Scotland.

———. 1995. "Selling and Processing Law: Legal Work at Franchise Law Firms." *Law and Society Review* 29: 703–729.

———. 1993. "Prepackaged Law: The Political Economy and Organization of Routine Work at Multi-Branch Legal Services Firms." Ph.D. dissertation, Northwestern University.

Wallace, J. E. 1995. "Corporatist Control and Organizational Commitment among Professionals: The Case of Lawyers Working in Law Firms." *Social Forces* 73: 811–839.

Index

Abbott, A., 3, 4, 130
Abel, R. L., 3, 12, 130, 137
Adultery, 9
Advertising, 1, 23, 41, 42; benefits, 52–54; costs to branch offices, 45–46; downside, 54; efficacy, 20; impact on work flow, 21; professional onus, 2, 12, 62; to select groups, 20, 52
Advertising strategies, 41–42, 69, 135; effect on revenues, 100, 108–109; price emphasis, 52; target markets, 20, 52
Alienation, 2, 87, 97, 111–112; *versus* entrepreneurialism, 132–134; of female attorneys, 116–117, 126–127
Aronson, R. L., 117
Arthur & Nelson (pseud.): advertising strategies, 41–42, 69, 108–

109, 135; attorney attitudes toward unionization, 119–127; attorney career paths, 94–97, 121; attorney competition within, 92; attorney turnover, 91–93, 112n. 2; branch office evaluations, 32; case types, 28, 69–70, 133; centralization of production, 112; compensation systems, 31–33, 50n. 1; computer systems, 43, 70; divorce specialization, 69–70; experts list, 64–65; future trends, 41, 136; health insurance, 116; hiring practices, 119; hours of operation, 116; incentive system, 94–97, 101; management, 99, 119–120; management attitudes toward unionization, 116; managing attorneys, 29–33, 119; maternity

About the Author

JERRY VAN HOY is Assistant Professor of Sociology at Purdue University. With a doctorate from Northwestern University, his research and other academic interests range from the political economy of legal work to the organization and operation of private governments. Van Hoy has published in journals serving the legal and sociological communities and is completing studies in both fields.